SURVIVING SEPARATION

GRAHAM MCFARLAND

**Understanding Family Law
Without Confusion**

"My Hope is That
This Guide
Will Offer You the Knowledge,
Confidence, and Clarity
You Need"

Graham McFarland

Copyright Notice

Copyright © 2025 by Graham McFarland. All rights reserved.

No part of this publication may be reproduced, distributed, or transmitted in any form or by any means, including photocopying, recording, or other electronic or mechanical methods, without the prior written permission of the copyright owner, except in the case of brief quotations embodied in critical reviews and certain other non-commercial uses permitted by copyright law.

For permission requests, write to the publisher

ISBN Number
978-1-7638393-1-1 Surviving Separation print
978-1-7638393-3-5 Surviving Separation Hard Cover
978-1-7638393-2-8 Surviving Separation Kindle
978-1-7638393-0-4 Surviving Separation eBook

Disclaimer The information in this book is for informational purposes only and does not constitute legal, financial, or professional advice.

CONTENTS

	Preface – Why I wrote this Book	1
1	The First Emotional Stages of Separation	5
2	Empowering Yourself Through Knowledge	15
3	Achieving the Right Mindset	25
4	Communicating with Your Children	38
5	Key Factors in Child Custody Decisions	46
6	How Long Does It Take to Resolve a Matter?	50
7	What is Mediation in Family Law?	57
8	What is Parental Responsibility?	62
9	When Do You Need a Family Lawyer?	71
10	How Do I Find the Best Lawyer for Me in Australia?	76
11	Do I Have to Go to Court?	84
12	What Factors are Considered?	90
13	When and How Child Support Starts.	97

14	Other Bills the Ex is Asking to Pay	103
15	Does Family Law System Protect Me from Violence?	108
16	How Do Domestic Violence Laws Vary from States?	116
17	Enhanced Protections for Victim Survivors of DV	125
18	Criminalising Coercive Control	133
19	How is Property and Assets Divided?	143
20	What Happens with Undeclared Assets?	149
21	Can I Relocate My Child After a Separation?	156
22	We Got Married, How Does This Change Things?	164
23	When and How Can You Get Divorced in Australia?	171
24	Getting Divorced After Being Married Overseas.	177
25	Traveling with Children After Separation.	181
26	The Different Roles and Positions in Court.	185
27	Helpful Resources.	194
28	"Hang in There"	204

"The Goal of This Book Is Not to Offer Legal Advice.

<u>*I Am Not a Lawyer,*</u>

And This Is Not a Substitute for Legal Counsel.

This Book Is a Collection of Common Conversations I've Had with Multitudes of Australian's Trying To...

Survive Separation".

Graham McFarland

Preface – Why I wrote this Book

My role, and the purpose of this book, is to fill that gap by giving you the knowledge and tools to better understand the system and how it impacts your life. Along the way, I will share insights into how Australian Family Law functions, explain some basic processes you may encounter, and offer practical tips to help you avoid common pitfalls.

However, I will also emphasise that every case is distinctly different, and what worked for someone else may not work for you. One of the most common areas I address as an advocate is **relationship breakdowns**.

Whether through divorce or separation of Marriage or "Defacto" relationships, the end of a relationship often is fraught with emotional and practical challenges. This book will walk you through what to expect when a relationship ends - what legal steps must be taken, the role of mediation, and how to protect your interests while keeping the best interests of any children involved front and centre.

I will also stress that clear communication during these times, not just with your former partner, but also with your legal representatives, support systems, and, most crucially, your children, is your main focus and road to success.

Parenting and child custody disputes are perhaps the most heart-wrenching and contentious issues in family law. As a parent, your primary concern is naturally your child's welfare.

The "**Family Law Act**" places the child's best interests at the core of its decisions but understanding what this means in practical terms can be difficult. We will explore the principles of shared parental responsibility, parenting plans, and how courts decide on living arrangements for children. I will also touch on the importance of focusing on your child's needs rather than getting caught up in the emotions of a legal battle with your former partner.

Another key topic is **financial and property settlements**. When a relationship ends, there is often a need to divide property, assets, and debts. While the law aims to achieve a just and equitable outcome, this does not always mean an equal division.

This book will guide you through the principles of property settlement, including how assets are assessed and the factors that courts consider when deciding how to divide property between separating couples.

Importantly, I will highlight how you can approach these discussions in a way that minimises conflict and promotes a fair resolution.

In some cases, **domestic violence** may be a factor in a relationship breakdown. This is a sensitive and urgent issue that demands immediate attention. I will discuss the protections available under Australian law, including intervention orders (also known as AVOs or restraining orders), and how the court takes allegations of domestic violence into account when decisions about children and property.

If you or someone you know is experiencing domestic violence, this book will provide guidance on what steps you can take to protect yourself and your family.

Throughout these discussions, I will also touch on the various **alternative dispute resolution** methods available. These options can often provide a less adversarial and more cost-effective way of resolving disputes. Wherever possible, it is worth considering these avenues before heading into a courtroom, which can be both emotionally and financially draining.

Family law is not static. It evolves with changes in society, legal precedents, and the ways we understand relationships and family dynamics. As we move forward, new challenges will arise, such as those posed by **international custody disputes**, **blended families**, and **grand-parental rights**.

While this book focuses on the core aspects of family law, it is important to remember that laws and attitudes shift over time. Staying informed and connected with legal professionals and support services is essential.

Ultimately, this book is about empowering you to take charge of *your family law journey*. Whether you are "in the midst" of a legal battle, contemplating separation, or simply seeking to understand your rights and responsibilities, my hope is that this guide will offer you the knowledge, confidence, and clarity you need.

Family law can be daunting, but with the right support, information, and mindset, it is possible to navigate it with dignity and achieve the best possible outcome for you and your family.

As you read through these pages, remember that you are not alone. Many have walked this path before you, and while no two journeys are identical, the collective experience of those who have come before can provide invaluable insights and support.

I am honoured to share what I have learned, and I hope that this book will serve as a helpful companion on your journey through family law.

"At All Times, Domestic Violence Is Not Okay,

and If in Immediate Danger
Please Call 000.

Otherwise, Call Your Local Police Station for
Assistance and Guidance"

Graham McFarland

| 1 |

The First Emotional Stages of Separation

Separation is not just a legal event or a change in living arrangements - it's an earthquake in the soul. The aftermath shakes every part of your identity, your routine, and your sense of safety.

One day, you have a partner who knows your secrets, dreams, and quirks; someone you confide in daily and build your life around. The next, they are gone, and the silence that follows is deafening.

For me, the initial days/months of separation were a descent into darkness. It wasn't just the absence of my partner but the realisation that the life I had planned, the future I had envisioned, was now gone. I wrestled with overwhelming anxiety, sleepless nights, and the sharp ache of not being apart from my children's life.

Looking back, it was like navigating a storm at sea without a compass, where every wave threatened to pull me under.

"Who Do You Turn To ...

When The Person You Always Turned To...

Is No Longer There?"

Graham McFarland

The Struggle to Adapt

We humans are creatures of habit. We find comfort in routines and the familiarity of relationships. When a relationship ends, especially one where intimacy was deep and constant, it's as if a part of your identity is torn away.

The mornings are the hardest. You wake up expecting to hear their voice, or instinctively reach for your phone to share something trivial, only to remember - there's no one on the other end anymore.

The loss of that daily connection left a void that I didn't know how to fill. Who do you turn to when the person you always turned to is no longer there? The absence is not just physical; it's emotional and psychological.

It's the little things - shared jokes, knowing glances, and the rhythm of a shared life - that linger like ghosts in your mind.

Separation from Children: A Unique Pain

For parents, the separation from children amplifies the pain. It's a wound that cuts deeper than words can express. The first weekend without my children was unbearable. Their laughter, their questions, their very presence - all absent.
I questioned everything: Was I a good enough parent? Would they resent me for the separation? Would they be, okay?

The anxiety was relentless. I found myself replaying moments from the past, wondering if I could have done something differently to avoid this. The guilt was a constant companion, whispering doubts in my ear.

I missed the bedtime stories, the hugs, and even the chaos of managing school drop-offs and packed lunches.

"I Found Myself Replaying Moments From the Past,

Wondering if I Could Have Done Something Differently to Avoid This"

Graham McFarland

The Ripple Effect

The fallout from separation doesn't just stay confined to the relationship - it seeps into every other part of your life. Friendships become strained as people take sides or avoid the discomfort of your pain.

In my experience I lost 100's of family members, friends, acquaintances, to many to bare. Their silence was deafening, something I didn't understand at the time, and it's been very hard to be forgiving.

Work becomes harder as your focus wavers under the weight of emotional exhaustion. Community events, once a source of joy, feel like reminders of what you've lost.

For me, this was a period where everything felt meaningless. The purpose I once found in work, parenting, and community vanished. It's not that I stopped caring; it's that I was so consumed by my own pain that I had nothing left to give.

The side effects were clear:

*irritability, a lack of patience,
and a tendency to withdraw from others.*

I found family events hit me the hardest. Coming from a large family, being active in my sibling's lives was part of my DNA. Especially when it came to my nieces and nephews. The pain in seeing them, with their small happy families, just brought more heart ache and poor behaviour from me.

I only wish one day they will comprehend this pain, and finally forgive me and engage with me again.

But amidst the darkness, there were flickers of light. I found myself drawn to helping others, not out of a sense of obligation, but because it gave me a reason to get out of bed. Contributing to my community became a lifeline, a way to rebuild my sense of self and purpose.

Engaging with thousands of strangers, guiding and listening to their own struggles gave me goals for tomorrow. But all of this was in the absence of my own family.

Pyrrhic Victories

In those early days, the separation felt like a battle - a fight for fairness, for dignity, for the right to be heard. Every argument and every legal proceeding felt like a small war, with victories and losses tallying up on an invisible scoreboard.

But over time, I realised that focusing on these skirmishes was a mistake.

The phrase *"Pyrrhic victory"* comes to mind. Pyrrhus of Epirus (Greece 318 BC) won a famous battle, but the cost of his victory was so great that it ultimately led to his downfall.

In the context of separation, this means that even if you "win" small battles - be it an argument, a legal point, or a moment of perceived vindication - you may lose something greater in the process:

Your Peace, Your Energy, And Your Focus on What Truly Matters.

During these days I really did not know what really mattered, in hindsight it slowed my growth for moving on to a better life.

Winning the battle is not the same as winning the war. The war - the bigger picture - is about healing, building a new life, and creating a future for yourself and your children. It's about choosing your battles wisely and understanding that some fights are not worth the cost.

Lessons from Sun Tzu
The ancient strategist Sun Tzu wrote...

"The Greatest Victory is That Which Requires No Battle."

This resonates deeply in the context of separation. So much of what we agonise over - who said what, who gets more, who seems to "win" - are distractions from the real goal... finding peace and stability.

I remember a turning point in my own journey when I decided to stop reacting to every provocation. Instead of engaging in endless disputes, I focused on what I could control - my own growth, my relationship with my children, and my contributions to my community.

It wasn't easy, but oh boy was it liberating.

Sun Tzu also said,

"Victorious Warriors Win First
and Then Go to War,
While Defeated Warriors Go to War First and Then Seek to Win."

This became my guiding principle. Winning first meant finding inner peace, setting my priorities straight, and refusing to let anger or bitterness dictate my actions.

*"I Needed to Focus On
Being the Best Version of ME,

So I Can Be the Best DAD
My Kids Deserve"*

Graham McFarland

Hope Beyond the Darkness

To anyone reading this, I want you to know that this time in your life is temporary. The pain you feel now, as overwhelming as it is, will not last forever.

Dreams may have been shattered, and life plans may have changed, but there is so much more waiting for you - things you cannot see yet, but they are there, just over the horizon.

Patience is your ally in this journey. Healing takes time, and so does rebuilding. Allow yourself to grieve, but don't let grief consume you. Focus on yourself, your growth, and your future. Surround yourself with people who uplift you, and don't be afraid to seek help when you need it.

Above all, don't be so hard on yourself. You're human, and humans struggle with change. But within that struggle is the seed of transformation. The war you're fighting is not against your ex-partner or the legal system - it's against despair, hopelessness, and fear... **"And that is a war you can win"**!

As I reflect on my own journey, I see how Sun Tzu's wisdom guided me through the chaos. The battles I chose to avoid saved me energy for the wars that mattered:

> *"Rebuilding my life, reconnecting with my children, and rediscovering my purpose".*

Today, I can say with confidence that while I may have lost a few battles along the way, I have won the war. And so will you.

*"Remember Brother,
She May Win These Little Battles,*

*But She Will Never Win
The War"*

Major Matthew McFarland CSM
Australian Regular Army Retired

| 2 |

Empowering Yourself Through Knowledge

When facing family law matters, such as divorce, child custody disputes, or property settlements, it's easy to feel overwhelmed by the legal complexities, emotional strain, and the sheer volume of decisions that need to be made.

However, there is a powerful tool that can help you navigate this challenging time with greater control and confidence: **knowledge**.

Understanding the legal process, your rights, and the options available to you is essential for making informed decisions that align with your best interests and those of your family.

Beyond the legal framework, it's equally important to focus on your personal health, relationships, and long-term goals to emerge from this period stronger and more empowered.

The Power of Knowledge in Family Law

Family law in Australia is designed to resolve disputes related to relationships, children, and financial matters in a fair and equitable way. However, the system can be complex and navigating it without proper knowledge can leave you feeling powerless.

The first step toward empowerment is **understanding the legal process**. This includes knowing the roles of the court, judges, lawyers, and other professionals who may be involved in your case.

For example, understanding the importance of mediation as a method for resolving disputes outside of court can not only save you time and money, but also reduce stress.

Knowing that the court's decisions regarding children are always guided by the **best interests of the child** helps you frame your approach to custody arrangements with a focus on cooperation and prioritising your child's well-being.

When you have a clear grasp of how property is divided and how spousal maintenance is calculated, you can enter negotiations or court proceedings with realistic expectations.

Informed decision-making also includes being aware of the options available to you. Should you pursue mediation or litigation? How can you ensure that your financial disclosures are accurate and complete?

By educating yourself about your rights and responsibilities, you minimise surprises and increase your ability to make decisions that are aligned with your long-term objectives.

Shifting Your Mindset: From Reactivity to Pro-activity

Knowledge, however, is just one aspect of empowerment. To fully navigate the family law process with confidence, you must also cultivate the right **mindset**.

During this time, it's natural to feel reactive responding to the actions of your ex-partner, legal proceedings, or court decisions. However, shifting from a **reactive** to a **proactive** mindset can transform your experience.

Being proactive means anticipating challenges and preparing for them rather than waiting for problems to arise. It involves setting clear goals for the outcomes you want and developing strategies to achieve them.

Instead of simply reacting to the demands of the court or your ex-partner, you take control of the process by working with your lawyer to create a plan that protects your interests.

This shift in mindset also includes focusing on what you **can control**, rather than dwelling on what is beyond your influence. You can't control the court's decisions, but you can control how you present your case, how you approach negotiations, and how you care for yourself and your children during this time.

By focusing on these aspects, you regain a sense of agency, which can greatly reduce stress and anxiety.

Prioritising Relationships and Communication

Amid the legal battles and emotional turmoil, it's easy to lose sight of the importance of maintaining healthy relationships. Whether it's your relationship with your children, friends, family, or even with your ex-partner, fostering positive communication and respect is essential.

If you have children, your relationship with them should remain your top priority. They are likely going through their own emotional journey during this time, and they need stability and reassurance from you.

Focusing on creating a safe, supportive environment for your children, even as you work through legal issues, can make a significant difference in their well-being and development.

Your relationship with your ex-partner, though changed, is also important to manage carefully—particularly if children are involved. It's natural to feel anger, frustration, or sadness toward your former partner, but keeping your interactions civil and cooperative is in the best interest of your children and can help the legal process move more smoothly.

In my journey, I lost all respect for my ex-partner, but I had to find a way to resolve my disappointment in them and find a way to at least respect the idea that they are still my children's parent too.

Practising **effective communication** and avoiding escalation of conflict will not only protect your mental health but also make it easier to reach mutually beneficial agreements.

Support from friends and family is equally crucial. Leaning on your support system can provide emotional relief, helping you to process feelings of grief, anger, or uncertainty.

However, it's important to ensure that the advice or opinions you receive from well-meaning friends and family align with your long-term goals and the legal advice from your lawyer.

*"To Fully Navigate the Family Law Process
With Confidence,*

*You Must Also Cultivate
the Right Mindset".*

Graham McFarland

Taking Care of Your Personal Health

Legal and emotional stress during family law disputes can take a toll on your **physical and mental health**. It's essential to prioritise self-care during this time. This means making time for activities that help you decompress, such as exercise, meditation, or hobbies that bring you joy.

Physical activity has been shown to reduce stress and improve mental health by releasing endorphins, which can help elevate your mood. For me it was boxing classes at my local 24-hour gym, especially after returning my children to their mother.

Sleep is another critical aspect of self-care. Poor sleep can exacerbate feelings of anxiety and depression, making it harder to cope with the pressures of legal proceedings. Establishing a bedtime routine and creating a peaceful sleep environment can improve the quality of your rest, helping you to stay focused and calm throughout the day. But remember, falling to sleep through indulging in alcohol, is not healthy or beneficial.

If the emotional strain becomes overwhelming, don't hesitate to seek professional help. Therapy or counselling can provide a safe space to process your emotions and develop coping strategies. A therapist can help you build resilience, improve communication skills, and maintain perspective during this challenging period.

In Australia, your GP can prescribe free counselling under the Medicare scheme. I always suggest parents to book an appointment with their GP, let them know what you have going through. Get a full health check, including blood tests.

Setting Long-Term Goals: Focusing on the Future

One of the most empowering things you can do during a family law dispute is to focus on your **long-term goals**. While the legal process may feel all-consuming in the short term, it's important to remember that this period is temporary. Setting clear, long-term goals helps you maintain perspective and ensure that your decisions today align with your vision for the future.

Long Term goals may include

Financial independence
Consider what steps you can take to build a stable financial future, including budgeting, career development, or seeking professional financial advice.

Healthy co-parenting
If you have children, work toward establishing a cooperative co-parenting arrangement that priorities their well-being and allows both parents to remain actively involved in their lives.

Personal growth

This period of change offers an opportunity for personal reflection and growth. Setting goals for self-improvement—whether through education, hobbies, or personal development—can help you rebuild and move forward in a positive direction.

Focusing on the future doesn't mean ignoring the challenges of the present, but it does allow you to approach the situation with a clearer sense of purpose.

By aligning your decisions with your long-term goals, you can emerge from this difficult time feeling empowered, rather than defeated.

My thoughts...

Navigating family law matters can be a difficult and emotionally draining experience, but with the right mindset, knowledge, and support, you can take control of the process and protect your interests.

Empowering yourself with knowledge of the legal system, shifting your mindset to proactive decision-making, maintaining healthy relationships, and prioritising your personal health are all essential elements of navigating this challenging time.

*"By Focusing on Long-Term Goals
And Remaining Resilient,*

*You Can Emerge from The Family Law Process Stronger,
More Confident,*

*And Ready to Embrace
The Next Chapter of Your Life".*

Graham McFarland

| 3 |

Achieving the Right Mindset

Navigating family law issues—whether they involve divorce, child custody, property settlements, or spousal maintenance—can be one of the most challenging periods in a person's life.

The stress, uncertainty, and emotional toll can feel overwhelming, leaving you struggling to cope with immediate concerns while worrying about the future. However, there's a crucial tool at your disposal to help you navigate these turbulent times.

How to Cultivate a Proactive Mindset

Knowledge

Empowering yourself through knowledge about the family law system, your rights, and the options available to you can shift your experience from one of helplessness to one of control. Yet, legal understanding is just one piece of the puzzle.

To truly thrive during and after a family law dispute, you must also focus on achieving the right mindset, maintaining relationships, prioritising personal health, and setting long-term goals. Let's explore how these elements combine to help you not only survive but thrive during family law challenges.

Achieving the Right Mindset

The emotional strain of a family law dispute, particularly when it involves children or significant financial changes, can lead to a reactive mindset. This is when you're constantly responding to crises, reacting to the actions of your ex-partner, or feeling blindsided by new legal developments.

Shifting from a reactive mindset to a proactive one is essential for navigating this period with a sense of agency and control. A proactive mindset focuses on what you can control rather than what you cannot. You may not be able to control the court's decisions, the actions of your ex-partner, or the pace of the legal process, but you can control your preparation, your responses, and your overall approach.

Educate Yourself

Take the time to understand your legal rights, the roles of professionals in the family court (such as judges, family consultants, and lawyers), and the options available to you (like mediation versus litigation).

When you're informed, you'll feel more confident and prepared.

Set Clear Objectives

Focus on your long-term goals. What kind of outcome do you want, not just for today but for your future? Whether it's financial security, shared parenting responsibilities, or maintaining a positive relationship with your children, having a clear vision will help guide your decisions.

Focus on What Matters

It's easy to get caught up in the emotional drama of a family law dispute, but it's crucial to focus on what truly matters—your well-being and the well-being of your children. Avoid getting distracted by minor conflicts or emotional provocations that could detract from your goals.

"By Proactively Setting The Tone for Your Actions And Decisions,

You'll Feel More in Control of The Process, Even When Circumstances Are Difficult".

Graham McFarland

Focusing on Relationships During This Time

Family law disputes can cause significant strain on relationships, especially those with your children, your ex-partner, and your support network. Yet, maintaining healthy and constructive relationships during this time is critical for your emotional health and the overall outcome of the situation.

Also be very aware, that during these times we often sort for comfort and support. It's common for separating partners to start a new relationship relatively quickly. Just be aware that time is needed to repair yourself, before committing to a new relationship.

It is often observed that people may attract a new relationship that really isn't the best outcome they need at the time, causing more anxiety and stress.

My number one rule, especially for men, do **NOT** start a new relationship for at least 6 months, possible a year for this exact reason!

Relationships with Your Children
If you have children, their well-being should be the top priority. Divorce or separation can be incredibly confusing and destabilising for children, so it's important to provide them with a sense of security and emotional support.

Communicate Honestly
Children are often more aware of what's happening than we realise. Be honest with them about the changes but frame the conversation in a way that's age-appropriate and reassuring. Let them know that both parents love them, and the separation is not their fault. And try stop using phrases like "I promise…".

Create Stability

Consistency and stability are crucial for children during family upheaval. Try to maintain their daily routines, school schedules, and activities to provide a sense of normalcy.

Co-Parent with Respect

While the relationship with your ex-partner may be strained, it's important to prioritise a cooperative co-parenting dynamic. Avoid speaking negatively about your ex-partner in front of your children, as this can create emotional confusion for them.

"It Is Often Observed…

That People May Attract a New Relationship
That Really Isn't the Best Outcome
They Need at The Time,
Causing More Anxiety and Stress.

My Number One Rule, Especially for Men,
<u>*Do NOT*</u>
Start a New Relationship For At Least 6 Months,
Or even A Year for This Exact Reason"!

Graham McFarland

Managing Your Relationship with Your Ex-Partner

Even though your romantic relationship with your ex-partner has ended, the way you manage your ongoing interactions will significantly impact the legal process and your emotional well-being, particularly if you're co-parenting.

Effective Communication

Communicate respectfully and directly about matters related to your children and any ongoing financial arrangements.

If face-to-face or direct conversation leads to conflict, consider communicating through email or a co-parenting app that structures communication in a neutral way.

Setting Boundaries

Clear boundaries are essential for reducing stress and conflict. Decide how you will handle communication, logistics around child custody, and other practical matters. When boundaries are respected, it reduces the emotional fallout from every interaction.

Leaning on Your Support System

Don't underestimate the importance of having a **support system** during this time. Whether it's friends, family, or professional support like a therapist or counsellor.

Surrounding yourself with people who care about you can make all the difference.

Reach Out

Don't be afraid to ask for help. Whether it's emotional support, practical assistance with childcare, or just someone listening to you venting, a support network can ease the burden of the situation.

Seek Professional Help

If you're struggling with emotional overwhelm or anxiety, consider seeing a therapist or counsellor. Family law disputes can trigger intense emotional reactions, and professional support can help you navigate these emotions healthily.

Prioritising Personal Health

Amid the legal and emotional turmoil, it's easy to let your personal health slide. Taking care of your physical and mental health is critical for coping with the stress and staying focused on your long-term goals.

Physical Health

Your body's response to stress can have a direct impact on how you handle family law challenges. Maintaining your physical health can help you stay resilient and manage stress more effectively.

Stay Active

Regular exercise has been shown to reduce stress, boost mood, and improve sleep. Whether it's a daily walk, yoga, or a workout at the gym, finding time to move your body can provide an emotional and physical release.

Healthy Eating

Stress can lead to unhealthy eating habits, such as binge eating or skipping meals. Focus on a balanced diet to keep your energy levels up and avoid the emotional roller coaster that poor nutrition can bring.

Prioritise Sleep

Stress and anxiety can often lead to poor sleep, which in turn exacerbates emotional distress. Establish a bedtime routine, limit caffeine and screen time before bed, and create a restful environment to help improve your sleep quality.

Mental Health

Family law disputes can take a toll on your mental health. It's important to practice **self-care** and seek professional help if necessary.

Mindfulness and Meditation

Mindfulness and meditation are powerful tools for reducing anxiety and staying present. Incorporating daily mindfulness exercises can help you manage stress and keep perspective during difficult moments.

Therapy and Counselling

Therapy can be an invaluable resource during family law disputes. A counsellor can help you process complex emotions, develop coping strategies, and maintain a positive outlook on the future.

Setting Long-Term Goals

One of the most empowering things you can do during a family law dispute is to focus on your **long-term goals**. While the immediate situation may feel all-consuming, it's important to remember that this is a temporary phase in your life.

Setting clear long-term goals will help you stay focused and make decisions that align with the future you want to build.

Financial Independence

One of the most significant changes during a divorce or separation is financial. Whether you've been financially dependent on your partner or are facing a significant change in income, focusing on achieving financial independence is key.

Create a Budget

Review your finances and create a realistic budget that reflects your post-separation financial situation. Include child support, spousal maintenance, and any legal fees in your calculations.

Seek Financial Advice

If you're unsure about managing your finances, consider working with a financial planner who can help you create a long-term strategy for financial stability.

Personal Growth

This period of change can also be an opportunity for personal growth. Think about what you want to achieve personally and professionally in the future.

New Opportunities

Consider returning to school, starting a new career, or pursuing hobbies and interests you may have put aside during your marriage. Personal growth can help you rebuild your identity and create a fulfilling future.

Focus on Healing

Give yourself time to heal emotionally and mentally from the divorce or separation. Personal growth is a gradual process, and by focusing on healing, you'll be better equipped to move forward with a positive outlook.

Remember

Navigating family law disputes is challenging, but with the right mindset, focus on relationships, commitment to personal health, and long-term goal setting, you can emerge from this process empowered and resilient.

By taking control of what you can, maintaining healthy communication, and prioritising your well-being, you can transform this difficult period into a time of growth and empowerment. Your future is in your hands, and by focusing on the bigger picture, you can create a better life for yourself and your family.

*"Family Law Disputes
Can Take a Toll on Your Mental Health.*

It's Important to Practice Self-Care

*And Seek Professional
Help If Necessary".*

Graham McFarland

| 4 |

Communicating with Your Children

Through Challenging Times Family separation is one of the most emotionally taxing experiences for parents and children alike. Navigating these waters with sensitivity and grace is critical, especially when communication with your children becomes a cornerstone of their emotional stability and your enduring connection with them.

In this chapter, I share insights from my own challenges in trying to maintain a relationship with my young children and offer practical advice for both custodial and non-custodial parents. The goal is to encourage healthy communication, minimise conflict, and prioritise the well-being of your children.

For the Custodial Parent

As a custodial parent, you are often the primary caregiver. With this privilege comes the profound responsibility to ensure your children maintain a healthy, ongoing relationship with their other parent.

This is not just a legal obligation—it is a moral one that places the child's best interests above personal grievances.

The Importance of Supporting Relationships

Children thrive when they feel loved and supported by both parents. Alienating the other parent, whether intentionally or unintentionally, can lead to long-term emotional challenges for your child. Studies show that children who maintain regular, positive contact with both parents tend to exhibit higher self-esteem, better academic performance, and fewer behavioural problems.

Best Practices for Communication

Here are some effective strategies custodial parents can adopt to support regular interaction between their children and the non-custodial parent

Encourage Regular Contact
Facilitate consistent visits, calls, or video chats, even if it's inconvenient for you. Children need this stability to maintain emotional connections. If your ex is really an issue as you believe, they will make the mistakes through selfishness and forgetfulness.

Provide Updates
Keep the other parent informed about significant events or milestones in your child's life, such as school performances, achievements, or health updates. I recommend that this is done through email, has context and does not become a conversation thread.

Stay Neutral
Avoid criticising or blaming the non-custodial parent in front of the children. Your words shape their perception and emotional bond with the other parent. Being the parent that doesn't criticise, will

pay dividends when the children get older. Your relationship will be stronger for it.

Be Flexible
Life happens, and plans can change. Being accommodating fosters goodwill and reduces tension.

Ways to Support Connection

Create Shared Traditions
Encourage children to share their special moments or traditions with the non-custodial parent. You must remember that with these moments, children want to share them with both parents, and grandparents.

Use Technology Wisely
Help younger children use video calls or shared apps like photo albums to stay in touch with the other parent. Place them in a quiet private environment, and don't get involved in the conversation. Set a period so it's not seen as been invasive, like 20 minutes for the call.

Send Updates
Work with your child to write letters or emails to their other parent if in-person contact is limited.

Handling Disagreements

Disagreements with the non-custodial parent are inevitable, but how you handle them will shape your child's emotional well-being. Here's how to manage conflict constructively…

Model Healthy Communication
Use calm and respectful language when discussing disagreements, whether in front of your child or in private. I often use the phrase, "treat it like a business conversation". You are not in a relationship with your ex anymore, so don't treat the communication like so.

Protect Your Child's Emotional Space

Avoid sharing adult issues, court orders, or negative opinions about the other parent with your child. Doing so can create undue stress and confusion. It is remarkable how much children will absorb and feel pressured about. Let them be children and leave the adult conversations and opinions away.

Emphasise Temporary Challenges

Reassure your children that difficulties are being addressed and do not diminish either parent's love for them. Your ex is still their father/mother, and you need to respect that. If in your eyes they are not great at being one, its now not your responsibility to educate them or challenge them on this. You are not their partner anymore.

For the Non-Custodial Parent

Being a non-custodial parent is undeniably challenging. It often feels as though your role is diminished, but your presence in your children's lives is vital.

Even small, consistent efforts make a big difference in maintaining a strong bond.

The Value of Persistence

Your relationship with your children is built on trust, time, and love. In moments when access is limited or strained, persistence is key. Children notice your efforts, even if they don't verbalise it. Over time, these small acts of love and consistency solidify your place in their lives.

In my experience, I was not aware of my children's observation of my efforts, for almost 5 years. Don't get me wrong, it was so important during those 5 years that I was that rock for my children, they appreciated it, they just never knew how to communicate how they felt about it.

Best Practices for Staying Connected to your Children

Stick to the Schedule

Honour agreed-upon visitation times or contact arrangements, no matter how difficult it might be. Your reliability sends a message of stability. This is more important for the children than for you or your ex.

Be Present

When you are with your children, focus entirely on them. Put away distractions and make them feel valued. Make sure you put that "Mobile phone" away. And when you have them, its not time for you to get babysitters and socialise, its parent time.

Respect Boundaries

Avoid criticising the custodial parent during visits or calls. Focus on creating a positive, nurturing environment. Especially don't quiz the children about your ex at all.

Ways to Stay Connected

Create Rituals

Develop simple rituals, like a shared bedtime story over the phone or regular "movie nights" during visits. I would set up the lounge room with basic mattress and sleeping bags, microwave popcorn and homemade milkshakes. Its important NOT to do this is bedrooms.

Send Tokens of Affection

Write letters, record voice notes, or send small gifts to remind your children of your love. An easy one for my daughter was sending flowers on special occasions like birthdays, or successes at school (not Valentine's Day). Just be mindful that whatever you write, rest assured the ex will be reading it, so stay neutral.

Support Their Interests

Stay involved in their hobbies, even from afar. Ask about their soccer games or school projects. Be engaged with the moments that they feel are important. I became a specialist at mindcraft!

Dealing with Disagreements

Disagreements with the custodial parent can feel particularly frustrating when they impact your time with your children. However, how you manage these conflicts influences your long-term relationship.

Avoid Escalation

Keep emotions in check and focus on problem-solving rather than assigning blame. Be very careful about your language.

Focus on the Children's Needs

Frame discussions around what's best for the children, not your grievances. This be a minefield. You opinion and your ex's opinion with what's in the best interest of the child can be so different. Express your opinion but do fall into the trap of critiquing the ex's version.

Leverage Support

Seek mediation or legal support when disagreements become recurring or unmanageable, ensuring any actions align with your child's best interests. This can be time consuming but its effective.

Managing Disappointment and Emotions

Both custodial and non-custodial parents experience moments of disappointment, whether it's a missed visit, a cancelled call, or a difficult conversation. It's crucial to navigate these feelings without involving your children

Why Emotional Conduct Matters

Poor emotional conduct—such as yelling, blaming, or guilt-tripping—can damage your relationship with your children over time. Children often internalise these conflicts, feeling torn between their love for both parents.

Recognise Temporary Setbacks
Remind yourself that setbacks, while painful, are not permanent. Focus on the long-term relationship you're building.

Lean on Your Support Network
Talk to trusted friends, counsellors, or support groups about your frustrations instead of venting to your children. But lie on the side of caution, they are there to listen while you vent, not to solve your problems with their opinions.

Model Resilience
Show your children how to handle disappointment gracefully. This not only protects their emotional well-being but also teaches them invaluable life skills.

The Role of Coercive Control Laws

Recent changes to NSW laws around coercive control emphasise the importance of eliminating manipulative or controlling behaviours in parenting dynamics. Coercive control can manifest in various ways, such as restricting communication between children and the other parent, using children as pawns, or withholding information about the child's life.

How to Avoid Coercive Control

Custodial Parents
Facilitate open communication and respect the non-custodial parent's rights. Avoid using children as leverage in disputes.

Non-Custodial Parents
Respect the custodial parent's boundaries and avoid excessive demands or guilt-inducing behaviour.

Understanding and adhering to these laws is not just a legal requirement; it's essential for fostering a positive and supportive environment for your children.

Focusing on the Future

During times of conflict or separation, it is crucial to prioritise the well-being of your children. By focusing on healthy communication, respecting boundaries, and prioritising emotional stability, you can establish a strong foundation for your relationship with your children, regardless of the challenges encountered.

It is essential to remember that your children's love for both parents is invaluable, and fostering that bond represents the highest form of care you can provide.

| 5 |

Key Factors in Child Custody Decisions

As a family law advocate, I am frequently asked by parents navigating separation or divorce about how child custody arrangements are determined.

In Australia, the Federal Circuit and Family Court of Australia (FCFCOA) is tasked with making decisions in the best interests of the child, a principle central to family law. Understanding what the court considers when making child custody (or parenting) orders can help parents approach this emotional and challenging process with more clarity.

The Paramount Principle: The Best Interests of the Child

Under the **Family Law Act 1975**, the overriding consideration in any child custody decision is the "best interests of the child". The court's primary focus is not on the desires of the parents but on what will best ensure the child's welfare and development.

The court considers two primary factors when determining what is in the child's best interests:

1. **The benefit of the child having a meaningful relationship with both parents**,
2. **The need to protect the child from harm**, which includes physical, emotional, and psychological harm.

These two factors are weighed carefully, with the protection of the child from harm always taking priority.

Other Key Factors Considered by the Court
Beyond these primary concerns, the court also considers a wide range of additional factors to tailor its decision to each family's unique circumstances.
Here are some of the most significant…

Parental Involvement and Capacity
The court looks at the level of involvement each parent has had in the child's life, both before and after separation. It assesses each parent's capacity to provide for the child's physical, emotional, and intellectual needs, including the ability to offer stability and support. This can include evaluating the parents' work schedules, living arrangements, and their willingness to make decisions jointly in the child's best interests.

The Child's Wishes
While the court always priorities the best interests of the child, it also considers the child's views, depending on their age, maturity, and understanding. The older and more mature the child, the more weight the court is likely to give to their preferences. This is often facilitated through a **family report** or interviews with the child conducted by an independent professional. There is **Not** a set age for this.

Family Violence and Safety
Protecting the child from harm, especially from family violence, is a crucial factor. If there is evidence of family violence, abuse, or any

risk to the child's safety, the court will place significant weight on this. It can lead to decisions that limit one parent's time with the child or impose strict conditions on how contact is supervised.

Relationship with Siblings and Extended Family

The court also considers the child's relationships with siblings and other significant family members, like grandparents. Maintaining these relationships can be an important part of fostering the child's sense of continuity and connection.

Practical Considerations

Practical considerations, such as how far apart the parents live from each other, the child's schooling, and the need for consistency in education and extracurricular activities, play a role in the court's decision. If parents live far apart, this may limit the amount of time a child can reasonably spend with each parent, especially during the school year.

Equal Shared Parental Responsibility vs. Time Spent

It's important to note the distinction between **parental responsibility** and the amount of time a child spends with each parent. In many cases, the court starts with the presumption of **equal shared parental responsibility**—meaning both parents have an equal say in major decisions regarding the child's education, health, and religion, unless this presumption is rebutted due to concerns like family violence.

However, equal shared parental responsibility does not mean equal time. While the court will consider arrangements for the child to spend **substantial and significant time** with both parents, this does not necessarily mean a 50/50 split of time. The court will look at what is practical and in the best interests of the child when deciding how much time the child spends with each parent.

What Parents Should Understand

Flexibility and Communication Are Key
Parents who can communicate effectively and put the child's needs first often have more successful outcomes. Courts encourage parents to agree on arrangements outside of court, where possible, as this tends to be in the child's best interests.

Each Case Is Unique
Child custody decisions are highly individualised. What works for one family may not work for another, which is why the court examines a variety of factors.

Parenting Plans and Consent Orders
Parents can negotiate their own custody arrangements through a **parenting plan** or formalise them through **consent orders**. If parents cannot agree, the court will make parenting orders after assessing the best interests of the child.

The FCFCOA ensures that custody arrangements prioritise the child's best interests. Each decision is personal, focusing on safety, well-being, and relationships with both parents. Understanding these factors helps parents make informed decisions for their child's future.

| 6 |

How Long Does It Take to Resolve a Matter?

One of the most common concerns for people navigating family law issues is how long the process will take. As a family law advocate, I often explain that the timeline for resolving a family law matter can vary widely depending on the complexity of the issues, the willingness of both parties to negotiate, and whether the matter ends up in court.

In Australia, the time-frame can range from a few months to several years, depending on these factors. Below, I'll break down the factors that influence how long it might take to resolve your family law matter and offer some tips for streamlining the process.

Factors That Affect the Timeline

Type of Family Law Matter
Different types of family law matters have different timelines. Some matters, such as divorce, are relatively straightforward and may take only a few months, while more complex issues such as property settlements or parenting disputes can take much longer.

Divorce

In Australia, the process for divorce itself is relatively straightforward. You must be separated for at least 12 months before applying for a divorce, and once you've applied, the court usually finalises it within a few months. If both parties agree, the process is quicker. If there are no disputes about property or children, the divorce can be resolved without much delay.

Property Settlements

If you and your ex-partner can agree on the division of property, it can be resolved fairly quickly, sometimes within a few months. However, if the property settlement is contested or involves complex financial arrangements such as businesses, trusts, or superannuation, it can take 12 months or more to finalise.

Parenting Matters

Parenting disputes can take longer to resolve, especially if the matter goes to court. If you and your ex-partner can agree on parenting arrangements through Family Dispute Resolution (FDR) or mediation, the process can be completed in a few months. If the matter goes to court, it can take 12-18 months or more for the court to make final orders, depending on the complexity of the case and the court's schedule.

Whether the Matter Goes to Court

One of the biggest factors that can impact the timeline is whether the matter needs to go to court. Court proceedings are generally much slower than out-of-court agreements due to court backlogs, the complexity of cases, and the time required to gather evidence and prepare for hearings.

Out-of-Court Resolution

If both parties are willing to negotiate and resolve their issues through mediation or **consent orders**, the process is much faster. For example, if you reach an agreement on parenting or property matters and submit **consent orders** to the court, it usually takes about **4-6 weeks** for the orders to be approved.

Court Proceedings

If negotiations fail and the matter goes to court, the process can take significantly longer. Court cases often involve multiple hearings, the gathering of evidence, and expert reports.

On average, it can take **12-24 months** for a family law case to go from filing to final orders. If the case is complex, it may take even longer.

Complexity of the Case

The complexity of your family law matter is another key factor. For example, a case involving high-value assets, businesses, or international elements will take longer to resolve than a case where the issues are more straightforward.

Similarly, cases involving family violence, substance abuse, or mental health concerns may require more time as the court considers additional evidence and expert reports.

Cooperation Between the Parties

The more cooperative both parties are, the quicker the matter can be resolved. If both parties are willing to communicate, compromise, and negotiate, the process can be shortened significantly.

On the other hand, if one or both parties are unwilling to cooperate or actively try to delay the process (for example, by withholding information or failing to attend mediation), the timeline can extend considerably.

*"By Seeking Early Legal Advice,
Cooperating with the Other Party,
and Considering Alternatives Like Mediation,*

You Can Help Streamline the Process and Reach a Resolution More Quickly".

Graham McFarland

General Timeline for Common Family Law Matters

Divorce
Approximately **4-6 months** after 12 months of separation.

Property Settlements (Out of Court)
If negotiated through mediation, typically **3-6 months**.

Property Settlements (Court)
If contested and goes to court, typically **12-24 months**.

Parenting Matters (Out of Court)
Through Family Dispute Resolution or mediation, typically **3-6 months**.

Parenting Matters (Court)
If contested and goes to court, typically **12-18 months**, but complex cases may take longer.

How to Speed Up the Process
While the time frame for resolving a family law matter can depend on many factors outside of your control, there are steps you can take to help move things along

Seek Early Legal Advice
One of the best ways to speed up the process is to seek legal advice early. A family lawyer can help you understand your rights and obligations and guide you on how to negotiate effectively. Early advice can also help you avoid mistakes that could cause delays later.

Consider Mediation or Family Dispute Resolution
Mediation and FDR are much faster than court proceedings. If you and your ex-partner can agree on key issues, you can reach a resolu-

tion within a matter of months, rather than waiting years for a court decision.

Be Prepared and Organised

Whether you're negotiating out of court or preparing for a court case, being organised can make a big difference. Have all the necessary documents, financial records, and evidence ready to present when needed. Delays often occur when one party doesn't provide the required information in a timely manner.

> *But be careful. I have seen so many try to influence a fast result, and all it does is influence long term pain.*

Keep Communication Open

The more you can cooperate and communicate with your ex-partner, the faster the process will be. Even if you disagree on certain issues, keeping communication lines open can help avoid unnecessary delays.

Agree to Interim Orders

If your case is going to court, you can still agree to **interim orders** on certain issues (such as parenting arrangements or financial support) while you wait for the final hearing. This can help stabilise the situation and prevent delays while the case progresses.

When Delays Are Inevitable

In some cases, delays are unavoidable, particularly if the matter is complex or involves serious disputes over parenting or finances. The courts are often overburdened, and there can be lengthy waiting periods for hearings.

While this can be frustrating, having legal representation and staying organised can help ensure that your case progresses as efficiently as possible.

My Thoughts

The time it takes to resolve a family law matter in Australia depends on the nature of the dispute, the complexity of the case, and the willingness of both parties to negotiate.

While some matters, like uncontested divorces or out-of-court agreements, can be resolved in a few months, others, particularly contested cases that go to court, can take years.

By seeking early legal advice, cooperating with the other party, and considering alternatives like mediation, you can help streamline the process and reach a resolution more quickly.

| 7 |

What is Mediation in Family Law?

Mediation is an increasingly popular method for resolving disputes in family law, particularly in matters related to divorce, child custody, and property settlement. It serves as an alternative to traditional court proceedings, offering a more collaborative and often less adversarial approach.

As a family law advocate, I often recommend mediation as a first step for separating couples who wish to reach an amicable agreement without the stress and expense of going to court.

Here's a closer look at what mediation is, how it works, and the benefits it can provide.

What is Mediation?

Mediation is a structured process where an impartial third party, known as a **mediator**, facilitates discussions between parties involved in a dispute. The mediator's role is to help both parties communicate effectively, identify their needs and interests, and explore potential solutions to their issues. Importantly, the mediator does not make decisions for the parties; instead, they guide the conversation to assist the parties in finding common ground.

In the context of family law, mediation can be used for a variety of issues, including:

Child custody arrangements
Determining where children will live and how parenting responsibilities will be shared.

Property settlements
Dividing assets and liabilities after separation or divorce.

Child support agreements
Establishing financial arrangements for the care of children.

How Does Mediation Work?

The mediation process typically involves several key steps

Preparation
Before the mediation session, parties may be required to gather relevant documents and information regarding their situation. They should consider their priorities and what outcomes they hope to achieve.

The Mediation Session
The mediation session itself can vary in length and format. Often, it takes place in a neutral location, and both parties, along with the mediator, will be present. The session generally includes

Opening Statements
Each party has the opportunity to express their perspective on the issues at hand.

Discussion
The mediator facilitates a dialogue between the parties, encouraging open communication and helping them explore their needs and concerns.

Private Meetings
At times, the mediator may meet privately with each party to discuss sensitive issues or concerns.

Negotiation
Throughout the session, the mediator assists the parties in negotiating possible solutions. They help identify options that meet the interests of both parties and facilitate brainstorming.

Agreement
If the parties can reach a consensus, the mediator will help them draft a **mediation agreement** that outlines the terms of their agreement. This document may include arrangements related to parenting, property, or financial obligations. It's important for both parties to review this agreement carefully.

Legal Finalisation
While mediation agreements are not legally binding on their own, they can be made legally binding by applying to the court for **consent orders**. This ensures that the agreement can be enforced by the court if necessary.

Benefits of Mediation
Mediation offers several advantages compared to traditional court proceedings

Cost-Effective
Mediation is typically less expensive than going to court. It can help avoid the high costs associated with lengthy litigation.

Time-saving
Mediation sessions are often scheduled more quickly than court hearings, allowing parties to resolve their disputes in a timely manner.

Control Over Outcomes
Mediation empowers both parties to have a say in the outcome. They can work collaboratively to create solutions that are tailored to their specific circumstances, rather than having a judge impose a decision.

Less Adversarial
The mediation process is designed to foster cooperation rather than confrontation. This approach can help maintain relationships, which is especially important in cases involving children.

Confidentiality
Mediation sessions are confidential, meaning that anything discussed during the process cannot be used against either party in court. This encourages open and honest communication.

Focus on Future Relationships
Mediation emphasises collaboration and understanding, which can lead to improved co-parenting relationships post-separation. This is particularly beneficial for families with children, as it sets a positive tone for future interactions.

When is Mediation Required?

In Australia, mediation is often required before parties can file for certain family law matters in court, particularly those related to children. The **Family Law Act 1975** mandates that parents attempt to resolve their disputes through family dispute resolution services before applying to the court for parenting orders.

There are exceptions to this requirement in cases involving family violence or urgent matters.

Choosing a Mediator
Selecting the right mediator is crucial for a successful mediation process. It's important to choose a mediator who is experienced in family law and understands the specific issues at hand.

Mediators can be found through family dispute resolution services, community organisations, or private practice. Many mediators are accredited and possess the necessary qualifications to facilitate discussions effectively.

My Thoughts!
Mediation offers a valuable alternative to court for resolving family law disputes. It promotes communication, cooperation, and creative problem-solving, allowing parents and separating couples to make decisions that are in their best interests and those of their children.

By understanding the mediation process and its benefits, families can navigate their separation or divorce with greater ease and a focus on maintaining healthy relationships.

If you are considering mediation, seeking guidance from a family law advocate can help you understand the process and prepare effectively for successful outcomes.

| 8 |

What is Parental Responsibility?

As a family law advocate, I often find that parents dealing with separation or divorce may not fully understand the concept of **parental responsibility**.

In Australia, parental responsibility goes beyond the day-to-day care of children—it's a legal framework that ensures both parents remain involved in important decisions about their child's upbringing, even if they are no longer together.

Parental responsibility is a fundamental concept in Australian family law that often causes confusion among parents going through separation or divorce. As a family law advocate, I frequently explain that parental responsibility refers not just to who the child lives with or how much time they spend with each parent, but to the broader responsibilities parents have when it comes to making important decisions about their child's life.

In Australia, **parental responsibility** is enshrined in the **Family Law Act 1975**, and it ensures that both parents remain involved in significant decisions about their child's upbringing, regardless of their relationship status.

Parental responsibility is not automatically altered by separation or divorce. Both parents retain full parental responsibility unless a court order says otherwise. The law assumes that it is in the child's best interests for both parents to share responsibility for these important decisions, even if the parents do not live together.

Equal Shared Parental Responsibility

In most cases, Australian family law presumes that **equal shared parental responsibility** is in the best interests of the child. This means that both parents have an equal say in major decisions concerning the child's life, and they must consult and agree on matters such as school, major medical treatments or procedures, religious upbringing, and changes to the child's living arrangements that affect their time with either parent.

*"**Parental responsibility** refers to the **legal duties, powers, responsibilities, and authority** that parents have concerning their child".*

It encompasses the major decisions that need to be made about a child's welfare, including:

Education
Deciding which school, the child will attend and other educational decisions.

Health care
Choosing medical treatments or healthcare providers for the child.

Religious upbringing
Deciding the child's religious or spiritual education.

Living arrangements
Deciding where the child will live or if they will move to a different location.

Parental responsibility is not just about day-to-day care (like bedtime routines or meals) but focuses on the major, long-term decisions that affect the child's development and well-being.

Equal shared parental responsibility does not necessarily mean that the child spends equal time with each parent, nor does it affect day-to-day decisions (which can typically be made by the parent with whom the child is spending time).

When it comes to big decisions—such as changing schools, major medical treatments, or relocating—the law expects both parents to cooperate and reach a mutual agreement.

When the Presumption Does Not Apply

While the starting point is usually equal shared parental responsibility, there are situations where this presumption can be **rebutted**.

If there are concerns about **family violence, child abuse**, or other factors that may put the child at risk, the court may decide that it's not in the child's best interests for both parents to share parental responsibility equally.

In these cases, the court may award **sole parental responsibility** to one parent. This gives the designated parent the authority to make decisions about the child's life without needing to consult the other parent.

Sole parental responsibility is usually granted in situations where the court believes it is necessary to protect the child or when one parent is unable or unwilling to participate in the decision-making process.

Day-to-Day Decisions

While parental responsibility focuses on major, long-term decisions, it's important to understand that the parent with whom the child is spending time typically makes the **day-to-day decisions**. This includes everyday matters like what the child eats, their bedtime, or their daily activities.

Day-to-day decisions do not require consultation with the other parent unless they have broader implications for the child's welfare. For example, choosing a child's activities for the weekend generally does not need the other parent's input, but choosing to enrol the child in a long-term activity that affects the child's schedule may require consultation.

Parental Responsibility and Court Orders

Parents are encouraged to agree on parenting arrangements and shared parental responsibility through **parenting plans** or **consent orders**. If parents cannot agree, the court can make **parenting orders** that define how parental responsibility will be shared or allocated.

Parenting Plan

This is a written agreement between parents, outlining how they will share parental responsibility and time with the child. It is not legally enforceable but can be a useful tool for parents who are able to communicate and agree on key issues.

Consent Orders

If parents agree, they can formalise their arrangements by applying to the court for a consent order, which is legally binding.

Parenting Orders

If parents cannot agree, the court will issue parenting orders that allocate parental responsibility based on what is in the best interests of the child.

There are two main types of parenting orders related to parental responsibility

Equal Shared Parental Responsibility Orders

The court can order that both parents retain equal shared parental responsibility, meaning that they must make major decisions about the child jointly.

Sole Parental Responsibility Orders

If the court finds that shared responsibility is not in the child's best interests (for example, in cases of family violence), it may award sole parental responsibility to one parent.

Parental Responsibility
vs.
Time Spent with the Child

It's important to distinguish between **parental responsibility** and the amount of **time** a child spends with each parent. These are two separate concepts

Parental responsibility

refers to making significant decisions about the child's welfare.

Time spent

refers to how much physical time the child spends with each parent.

Even if one parent has **primary custody** (the child lives with them most of the time), both parents can still share **equal parental responsibility**, meaning they are both involved in making major decisions about the child.

Conversely, if one parent is awarded sole parental responsibility, the other parent may still have regular visitation or time with the child, but they may not have a say in major decisions.

What Happens If Parents Disagree?

If parents who share parental responsibility cannot agree on a major decision (such as schooling or health care), they are encouraged to resolve their dispute through **mediation** or **Family Dispute Resolution**. These processes aim to help parents come to an agreement without going to court.

If mediation is unsuccessful, parents can apply to the court for a **parenting order** to resolve the dispute. The court will then decide based on what is in the best interests of the child.

Legal Implications of Parental Responsibility

Wills and Inheritance
Parents with parental responsibility are typically considered the legal guardians of their children, which can have implications for issues like inheritance or appointing a guardian in a will.

Medical Decisions
Both parents with parental responsibility must consent to significant medical procedures for their child, except in cases where the court has ordered sole parental responsibility.

Travel and Relocation

If a parent wishes to relocate with the child, they must usually obtain the other parent's consent or a court order, as this is considered a major decision affecting the child's life.

Can Parental Responsibility Be Changed?

Yes, parental responsibility can be changed if circumstances change, or if the arrangement is not working in the child's best interests. Either parent can apply to the court for a **variation** of a parenting order. However, the court will require evidence that the change is necessary and that it will benefit the child.

For example, if one parent with shared responsibility moves overseas or is no longer involved in the child's life, the other parent may seek sole parental responsibility.

My thoughts!

Parental responsibility in Australia is about much more than where a child lives or how much time they spend with each parent. It is the legal framework that ensures both parents remain involved in making major decisions about their child's welfare, education, health, and overall upbringing.

The law generally presumes that equal shared parental responsibility is in the child's best interests, though this can be rebutted in cases involving family violence or other serious concerns. If you are unsure about your parental responsibilities or how they apply in your situation, seeking legal advice is crucial to ensure that you understand your rights and obligations as a parent.

In conclusion, parental responsibility is a fundamental concept in Australian family law that ensures both parents remain involved in important decisions about their child's life, regardless of their relationship status.

Equal shared parental responsibility is the default position, but in cases where the child's safety is a concern, the court may award sole parental responsibility to one parent. Understanding this distinction and knowing how to navigate these responsibilities can help parents better support their child's well-being after separation.

*"Parental Responsibility Is A
Fundamental Concept in Australian Family Law.*

*It Ensures Both Parents
Remain Involved in Important Decisions*

*About Their Child's Life,
Regardless Of Their Relationship Status".*

Graham McFarland

| 9 |

When Do You Need a Family Lawyer?

As a family law advocate, I'm often asked whether someone needs to hire a family lawyer when facing legal issues related to separation, divorce, or parenting. While some family law matters can be resolved without legal representation, there are situations where having a family lawyer can be invaluable.

Here's a guide to understanding when it's essential to seek professional legal help in Australia.

While it's possible to handle some matters independently, certain situations require expert legal guidance to protect your rights and ensure the best possible outcome.

Below are key instances where it's advisable to engage a family lawyer

Divorce and Property Settlements
If you're going through a divorce or separation, a family lawyer is often necessary to ensure that your financial interests are protected, particularly when it comes to property settlements. The division of assets, including property, savings, superannuation, and debts, can be

complex. A lawyer can help negotiate a fair settlement and ensure that any agreement complies with Australian family law.

Even if you and your ex-partner agree on how to divide assets, a lawyer can formalize the agreement by drafting a binding financial agreement or consent orders, which makes the agreement legally enforceable. This reduces the risk of future disputes.

Child Custody and Parenting Orders

If you and your ex-partner cannot agree on child custody arrangements, or if there is a dispute about who the child will live with or how much time they will spend with each parent, a family lawyer is essential. Child custody disputes are highly emotional, and legal expertise is crucial in ensuring that your child's best interests are upheld.

A family lawyer will guide you through the process of obtaining parenting orders or a parenting plan and represent you in court if necessary. They will help you understand what the Federal Circuit and Family Court of Australia considers when making custody decisions, including the child's best interests and any issues related to family violence or abuse.

Family Violence and Protection Orders

In cases of domestic or family violence, having a family lawyer is critical. They can help you apply for a Family Violence Intervention Order (also known as an Apprehended Domestic Violence Order, or ADVO), which provides legal protection from a violent or abusive partner. A lawyer can ensure that your rights are protected and that the order is enforced.

Similarly, if you have been wrongly accused of domestic violence and are defending against an intervention order, a lawyer can provide the necessary legal defence to protect your rights.

Disputes Over Superannuation

Superannuation can be a significant asset in family law property settlements, and it's often overlooked. Superannuation splitting is a complex area of law that requires expert advice.

A family lawyer can ensure that the division of superannuation is handled correctly and in line with legal requirements, which can make a significant difference to your financial future after divorce.

International Family Law Issues

If your family law matter involves international aspects—such as relocation of children overseas, enforcement of overseas custody or divorce orders, or international property—then legal advice from a family lawyer with experience in international family law is crucial.

The complexities of dealing with laws across different jurisdictions require expertise that only a lawyer can provide.

Situations Where Legal Representation May Not Be Necessary

There are times when you might not need a family lawyer, particularly if both parties are cooperative, and the issues are straightforward.

Mutual Agreement on Parenting Arrangements

If you and your ex-partner can agree on parenting arrangements for your children, you may not need a lawyer to go to court. Many parents can come to an agreement through negotiation or family dispute resolution (mediation).

While it's still advisable to have the agreement formalised with a parenting plan or consent orders, this can often be done without going through the court system.

Simple Divorces

If you have no children and no joint property to divide, a simple divorce application may not require legal representation. The divorce process in Australia is largely administrative, and if both parties agree, it can be handled without a lawyer.

However, it's still a good idea to seek advice if you're unsure about the process.

Family Dispute Resolution

In Australia, before going to court for parenting or property matters, parties are usually required to attempt Family Dispute Resolution, unless there are safety concerns such as family violence.

Family Dispute Resolution is a mediation process aimed at resolving disputes without the need for litigation. In many cases, mediation can lead to a mutual agreement, and while a lawyer can provide advice during the process, you may not need full legal representation.

What to Keep in Mind

Legal Advice Early Can Prevent Bigger Problems Later

Even if you're handling most of your family law issues independently, getting initial legal advice can save you time, money, and stress later. A family lawyer can help you understand your rights and obligations and can point out potential issues that may arise.

You May Qualify for Legal Aid

If you're worried about the cost of hiring a family lawyer, it's worth checking if you qualify for Legal Aid. Legal Aid offers free or reduced-cost legal services to those who meet certain financial criteria and are dealing with family law issues, particularly when children are involved.

Court Isn't Always Necessary

Going to court is often seen as the last resort in family law disputes. Many matters can be resolved through negotiation, mediation, or arbitration.

However, if court becomes necessary, having a family lawyer by your side is crucial to navigating the process and ensuring your voice is heard.

In conclusion, while you may not always need a family lawyer for every aspect of your separation or divorce, there are many situations where their expertise is crucial.

From complex property settlements to child custody disputes, a family lawyer can provide guidance, representation, and peace of mind during some of the most challenging moments of your life.

Knowing when to seek legal help can make all the difference in achieving a fair and positive outcome for you and your family.

| 10 |

How Do I Find the Best Lawyer for Me in Australia?

Finding the right lawyer for your family law case can make all the difference, especially during emotionally charged situations like divorce, child custody, or property settlements.

In Australia, many lawyers practice family law, but choosing the one that best suits your needs depends on several factors. Here's how to find the best lawyer for you

Search for a Family Law Specialist
Specialisation is key

Family law can be complex and unique, so it's important to find a lawyer who specialises in family law matters. These lawyers are familiar with the Family Law Act, legal procedures, and nuances related to property settlements, child custody, spousal maintenance, and more.

Accredited specialists

Look for lawyers who are accredited family law specialists. These professionals have undertaken additional training and are recognised as experts in the field.

Consider Experience and Expertise

Relevant experience

Ensure that the lawyer has experience handling cases similar to yours. For example, if your case involves complex financial settlements, make sure the lawyer is experienced in dealing with high-net-worth property divisions.

Reputation matters

Ask for referrals from people you trust or check online reviews. Lawyers with strong reputations in the community often have proven track records of success and a good rapport with clients.

Evaluate Communication and Compatibility

Comfort level

You should feel comfortable with your lawyer. Family law matters are personal and often emotional, so it's important to have a lawyer who listens, understands your concerns, and communicates clearly.

Availability

Make sure the lawyer is available to handle your case and isn't over-committed. You want someone who will give your case the attention it deserves.

Assess Costs and Transparency

Transparent fees

Legal fees can vary significantly depending on the lawyer's experience and the complexity of your case. Some lawyers charge an hourly rate, while others offer flat fees for certain services.

Make sure you understand the lawyer's fee structure before committing.

Legal Aid
If you're facing financial difficulties, ask if the lawyer offers Legal Aid services or other flexible billing arrangements.

Consult Professional Directories

Law Society directories
Each state and territory in Australia have a Law Society that maintains a list of accredited family law specialists. These directories are a great starting point for finding qualified lawyers in your area.

What Should I Ask My Lawyer During My First Consultation?

Your first meeting with a lawyer is a crucial step in determining whether they are the right fit for your case. During this consultation, it's important to ask the right questions to assess their experience, approach, and how they can help with your specific situation.

Here are some questions to consider

What Is Your Experience in Family Law?
Ask the lawyer how many years they've practised family law and whether they have handled cases like yours. This will give you an idea of their expertise and track record.

What Approach Do You Take in Family Law Cases?
Some lawyers emphasise mediation and negotiation, while others may be more aggressive litigators. Depending on your goals (amicable

settlement versus court battle), find out what their approach is and whether it aligns with your preferred strategy.

What Are My Legal Rights and Options?

Ask for an explanation of your legal rights and what options are available to you. A good lawyer will help you understand your entitlements in matters like property division, child custody, or spousal maintenance.

What Are the Likely Outcomes of My Case?

While no lawyer can guarantee an outcome, they should be able to give you a realistic assessment of what you can expect based on their experience and your specific circumstances.

How Long Will the Process Take?

Ask about the expected timeline for your case. Understanding the typical duration of family law cases like yours can help you plan emotionally and financially.

What Will It Cost?

Be sure to get a clear understanding of the costs involved. Ask about the lawyer's billing structure (hourly vs. flat fees) and whether there are any additional costs, such as court fees or expert reports.

What Should I Bring or Do Next?

Ask the lawyer what **documents** or information you should provide to strengthen your case. This could include financial records, communication with your ex-partner, or details of your assets.

When Should I Get Legal Advice for a Family Law Matter?

The sooner you seek legal advice for a family law matter, the better. Family law issues can have long-lasting consequences, and early legal advice helps you understand your rights and responsibilities, avoid mistakes, and navigate the complexities of the legal system. Here's when you should seek legal advice

Before Separation or Divorce

If you're considering separating from your spouse or partner, it's a good idea to get legal advice before making any decisions. A lawyer can help you understand your rights regarding property division, child custody, and spousal maintenance, and guide you on protecting your financial interests.

When Negotiating Parenting Arrangements

If you and your ex-partner are negotiating parenting arrangements, legal advice ensures that the agreement is fair and, in your child's, best interests. It's especially important to seek advice if there is disagreement over custody or if family violence is involved.

If Domestic Violence Is Involved

If you are experiencing domestic violence or feel unsafe, it's crucial to seek legal advice immediately. A lawyer can help you apply for protection orders and advise you on the best steps to ensure your safety and the safety of your children.

When Dividing Property and Finances

Whether you're dividing property after a separation or negotiating a financial settlement, it's important to seek legal advice.

A lawyer can help ensure that the division is just and equitable, especially if the assets involve complex financial arrangements, businesses, or superannuation.

When Drafting or Reviewing Agreements

Even if you and your ex-partner are on good terms and negotiating your own financial or parenting agreements, it's a good idea to have a lawyer review the documents before signing.

A lawyer can ensure the agreement complies with the law and is legally enforceable.

When Court Proceedings Are Involved

If negotiations break down and court proceedings are likely, getting legal advice early will help you prepare your case. A lawyer will guide you through the litigation process and represent your best interests in court.

When Your Circumstances Change

If there is a significant change in your circumstances (such as a new job, relocation, or changes in your child's needs), it's wise to seek legal advice to adjust existing court orders or agreements.

My Thoughts!

Finding the best lawyer for your family law matter in Australia involves searching for someone who specialises in family law, has relevant experience, communicates effectively, and offers transparent pricing.

During your first consultation, asking about their experience, approach, and fees will help you assess whether they are the right fit for your case.

Finally, seeking legal advice early—before separation, during negotiations, or when dealing with complex issues like domestic violence or property division—will help you avoid mistakes and protect your rights throughout the process.

"During this Consultation,

*it's Important to Ask the Right Questions
to Assess Their Experience,
Approach,*

*and How They can Help with Your
Specific Situation".*

Graham McFarland

| 11 |

Do I Have to Go to Court?

As a family law advocate, I am frequently asked by individuals whether they must go to court to resolve their family law issues. The good news is that, in Australia, you don't always have to go to court.

In fact, court is often seen as the last resort for resolving family disputes, and there are several alternatives that can help you reach an agreement without the stress, cost, and time of a court battle.

Here's what you need to know about whether court is necessary, and what your options are for resolving family law matters outside of the courtroom.

When Court May Not Be Necessary

In many family law cases, especially those involving parenting arrangements or property settlements, parties can resolve their disputes outside of court through mediation or negotiation. The Australian family law system encourages parents and separating couples to attempt to reach an agreement themselves before turning to the courts.

Family Dispute Resolution (FDR)

In most cases involving children, the law requires that separating parents attempt FDR before they apply to the court for parenting orders. FDR is a form of mediation where a neutral mediator helps parents work out their disagreements about child custody and parenting arrangements.

FDR allows parents to focus on the best interests of their children and often leads to more amicable outcomes. Agreements reached in FDR can be formalised through a parenting plan or consent orders, both of which can be made legally binding.

FDR is not required if there are concerns about family violence or child abuse, or if the matter is urgent. In such cases, the court may need to be involved immediately to ensure the safety and well-being of the child.

Parenting Plans and Consent Orders

Even if you and your ex-partner can reach an agreement on your own, it's a good idea to formalize your arrangements with a parenting plan or consent orders. A parenting plan is a written agreement between parents about the care of their children, and while it's not legally enforceable, it provides a clear framework for both parties.

If you want the agreement to be legally enforceable, you can apply to the Federal Circuit and Family Court of Australia for consent orders. This process does not require a court hearing, and it allows both parties to have a formal agreement without the need to go to court.

Negotiation of Property Settlements

For property and financial matters, many couples can resolve issues through negotiation, either directly between themselves or with the help of a lawyer. If you reach an agreement, you can formalise it through a binding financial agreement or consent orders.

Like parenting agreements, consent orders for property settlements can be submitted to the court without the need for a hearing.

When You Might Need to Go to Court

While many family law matters can be resolved outside of court, there are certain situations where court intervention is necessary.

No Agreement Can Be Reached

If you and your ex-partner cannot agree on critical issues—such as child custody, financial arrangements, or the division of assets—despite attempts at negotiation or mediation, you may need to apply to the court for a decision.

The court will consider the evidence presented by both parties and make a ruling based on the best interests of the children or the fairness of the property settlement.

Urgent or Complex Cases

In some cases, urgent or complex issues may require immediate court intervention.

For example, if there is a risk of family violence or child abduction, or if one party is trying to hide assets or dispose of property, the court can issue orders to protect the child or property. In such cases, it's important to seek legal advice and apply to the court as soon as possible.

Family Violence or Abuse

If there is evidence of family violence or child abuse, court involvement may be necessary to protect the safety of the children or one of the parents.

While FDR is typically required before applying for parenting orders, cases involving violence or abuse are exempt from this requirement, and the court can make urgent orders to safeguard the child or the victimised parent.

Contested Divorce or Financial Settlements

In some situations, one party may contest the divorce or the terms of the financial settlement, in which case the court will need to decide.

This can occur if there is disagreement about the division of assets, spousal maintenance, or the valuation of property. In these cases, the court's intervention is needed to ensure a fair and legally binding resolution.

What to Consider Before Going to Court

Court Is a Last Resort

Court can be a time-consuming, expensive, and emotionally draining process. It is often best reserved for cases where no agreement can be reached, or where there are serious concerns about safety or fairness.

Before going to court, consider whether mediation or negotiation could help you resolve the issue.

Legal Representation Is Key

If you do need to go to court, having legal representation is critical. A family lawyer can help you present your case effectively, ensure your rights are protected, and advocate for your interests. Without a lawyer, navigating the court system can be daunting.

Consent Orders Are Faster and Cheaper

If you can reach an agreement with your ex-partner, applying for consent orders is usually much faster and cheaper than going to court.

Consent orders offer the same legal enforce-ability as court orders but without the need for lengthy hearings.

My Thoughts!

In most cases, you don't have to go to court to resolve your family law matter in Australia. Mediation, negotiation, and consent orders provide effective ways to settle disputes without the need for lengthy court proceedings.

However, in cases involving violence, urgency, or significant disagreements, court intervention may be necessary to protect your rights and ensure a fair outcome. Understanding your options and seeking legal advice early can help you avoid the stress and cost of going to court, while ensuring the best possible outcome for you and your family.

*"Understanding Your Options
and Seeking Legal Advice Early,*

Can Help You Avoid the Stress and Cost of Going to Court,

While Ensuring the Best Possible Outcome,

*For You
And
Your Family".*

Graham McFarland

| 12 |

What Factors are Considered?

Child custody, or parenting arrangements, is one of the most critical issues following a separation or divorce. As a family law advocate, I often help parents navigate this complex process, emphasising that the primary goal of the court is to ensure that decisions are made in the best interests of the child.

The **Federal Circuit and Family Court of Australia (FCFCOA)** considers a wide range of factors to determine what those best interests are. Understanding these factors can help parents better prepare and focus on what truly matters: the well-being of their children.

The Best Interests of the Child

The guiding principle for the court when deciding child custody matters is the best interests of the child. This is enshrined in the Family Law Act 1975, which sets out the considerations the court must consider. The court's objective is to ensure that children maintain a meaningful relationship with both parents while also protecting them from harm.

When assessing what is in the best interests of the child, the court looks at two primary considerations:

1. *The benefit to the child of having a meaningful relationship with both parents.*

2. *The need to protect the child from harm, including physical or psychological harm, and being exposed to abuse, neglect, or family violence.*

Of these two considerations, the need to protect the child from harm takes priority.

Key Factors Considered by the Court

In addition to the primary considerations, the FCFCOA assesses a wide range of other factors to decide on the most appropriate custody (or parenting) arrangements.

These factors include:

The Child's Relationship with Each Parent

The court will examine the nature and quality of the relationship the child has with each parent, as well as with other important people in their life, such as grandparents or siblings.

A strong and positive bond with both parents is seen as beneficial, and the court will typically want to preserve that unless there are concerns about the child's safety or well-being.

Willingness to Facilitate a Relationship with the Other Parent

The court values cooperation between parents. It looks at whether each parent is willing to encourage and support the child's relationship with the other parent. If one parent is seen as trying to alienate the child from the other parent or refusing to facilitate contact, this could negatively impact their case for custody.

The court generally favours shared parenting responsibilities unless there are valid reasons not to.

The Views of the Child

While the child's views are not the deciding factor, they are taken into consideration, especially if the child is mature enough to express their preferences. The weight given to the child's views depends on their age, maturity, and level of understanding.

For example, an older child's wishes might carry more weight than a very young children, though the court will still evaluate whether those views align with the child's best interests.

Practical Considerations

The court will consider the practicalities of the proposed parenting arrangements, including...
- The distance between the parents' homes.
- The child's schooling and educational needs.
- The child's extracurricular activities and how they will be affected.
- The ability of the parents to cooperate and manage shared responsibilities like school drop-offs, medical appointments, and other day-to-day needs.

The Child's Age, Maturity, and Needs

Different children have different needs based on their age, emotional maturity, and stage of development. Younger children may require more frequent contact with both parents, while older children may have more complex educational and social needs that should be considered in parenting arrangements.

The court also assesses any special needs the child may have, such as medical or psychological care.

The Impact of Family Violence or Abuse

If there has been any history of family violence or child abuse, this will be a significant factor in the court's decision. The court is committed to ensuring the child's safety, and any evidence of physical, emotional, or psychological harm will be closely scrutinised.

The presence of family violence can lead to decisions that limit or restrict a parent's time with the child, especially if there is a concern that the child may be at risk.

Each Parent's Capacity to Provide for the Child's Needs

The court will look at each parent's ability to provide for the child's emotional, physical, and developmental needs.

This includes factors such as:
- The parent's mental and physical health.
- The parent's financial situation and ability to provide a stable home environment.
- Each parent's ability to meet the child's daily needs, including their ability to make appropriate decisions regarding the child's welfare, education, and health care.

Any History of Drug or Alcohol Abuse

If a parent has a history of substance abuse, this may impact the court's decision on custody arrangements. The court may take measures to protect the child, such as limiting contact with the parent, requiring supervised visits, or making orders for the parent to seek treatment.

Cultural Background and Identity

The court may consider the child's cultural background, including their Aboriginal or Torres Strait Islander heritage, and the importance of maintaining connections with their cultural community. The court seeks to respect the child's cultural identity and ensure that the parenting arrangements support the child's cultural needs.

Parental Responsibility

The court typically starts with the presumption that both parents should have equal shared parental responsibility. This means that both parents should jointly make decisions about the child's major long-term issues, such as education, health care, and religious upbringing.

However, this presumption can be rebutted if there are concerns about family violence, abuse, or the inability of the parents to cooperate effectively.

It is important to understand that equal shared parental responsibility does not mean that the child will necessarily spend equal time with each parent. The court will evaluate whether equal time is practical and, in the child's, best interests. If it is not, the court may decide that the child should spend substantial and significant time with both parents, which might include weekends, holidays, and special occasions, even if the child spends more time with one parent.

The Role of Family Reports and Experts

In cases where the court is unsure of the best arrangements for the child, it may order a family report or seek input from an independent children's lawyer.

A family report is prepared by a psychologist or social worker who assesses the family dynamics and provides recommendations to the court about the best parenting arrangements for the child. The court often gives significant weight to these expert reports.

Reaching Agreements Outside of Court

While the court plays a central role in determining child custody arrangements when parents cannot agree, it's often preferable for parents to reach agreements outside of court through mediation or Family Dispute Resolution (FDR).

Parents who can negotiate and cooperate are often better able to tailor arrangements to their child's needs and avoid the stress, time, and cost of a court battle. These agreements can then be formalised through consent orders, making them legally binding.

My Thoughts!

When determining child custody arrangements, the Federal Circuit and Family Court of Australia considers a range of factors to ensure that decisions are made in the best interests of the child. These factors include the child's relationship with each parent, the willingness of parents to cooperate, practical considerations, and the safety and welfare of the child.

Understanding these factors can help parents focus on what the court values most: the child's well-being, safety, and continued relationship with both parents.

By prioritising these considerations, parents can navigate the process with a clearer understanding of what's important and how to achieve the best outcomes for their children.

*"It's Important to Note
That Equal Shared Parental Responsibility*

Does Not Necessarily Mean

*That The Child Will Spend
Equal Time with Each Parent".*

Graham McFarland

| 13 |

When and How Child Support Starts.

Understanding child support is crucial for ensuring that your children are properly supported after a separation or divorce. Here's a breakdown of the key points, based on Australian family law.

When Does Child Support Start?

Child support typically begins when parents separate, and one parent becomes responsible for most of the child's care. However, the exact start date can vary depending on the situation. Child support can be assessed informally between parents or formally through Services Australia (Child Support), which oversees the process.

Child support typically begins as soon as a child's primary care arrangements are determined after separation or divorce. This can occur in several scenarios

Separation of Parents

If parents separate, the parent who has primary care of the child may apply for child support from the other parent. The obligation for child support arises from the moment the parents separate, even if there is no formal arrangement in place yet.

This means that if you have separated but have not yet finalised custody or care arrangements, you can still seek child support.

Establishment of Care Arrangements

Child support becomes more formalised once there are agreed-upon care arrangements for the child. This could include the primary residence of the child or shared custody arrangements.

The parent with whom the child primarily resides can apply for child support to help cover the costs of raising the child.

Child's Age

Child support is generally applicable until the child turns **18 years old**. However, if the child is still in secondary education when they turn 18, parents may continue to provide support until the completion of their education.

In such cases, parents can agree on a continuation of support or seek a court order to formalise it.

In most cases, child support will start from either

- The date the parents agree upon if they arrange it privately.
- The date the application for child support is lodged with Services Australia, or from a specified earlier date if applicable under special circumstances.

How is Child Support Worked Out?

The calculation of child support is based on several factors, including the income of both parents, the care arrangements for the child, and the costs associated with raising a child.

Income Assessment
The Child Support Agency (CSA) uses the income of both parents to calculate child support payments. Each parent's income is considered in the formula to ensure that support is equitable.

Parents are required to provide evidence of their income, which may include payslips, tax returns, or business financial statements.

Care Arrangements
The amount of time each parent spends with the child significantly impacts the child support calculation. The formula considers the percentage of care each parent provides

If one parent has primary care (more than 65% of the time), they will likely receive child support from the other parent. If the care is shared equally (50/50), the amount of child support may be reduced or eliminated, depending on the parents' incomes.

"The process of determining child support in Australia is designed to be fair and considers various factors".

The Basic Formula Used by Services Australia Incorporates

Income of both parents
Both parents' taxable income is considered, minus a self-support amount that covers the parent's basic living costs.

Percentage of care

How much time the child spends with each parent directly affects the calculation. If both parents share care equally, child support may not be required or could be minimal.

Cost of raising children

This is determined based on the age and number of children. The Australian government has a cost-of-children table that calculates a child's expenses according to their age.

For example, a parent earning a higher income but who has the child less frequently may be required to pay more child support than the lower-income parent with primary care.

What Parents Should Know

Adjustments Over Time

Child support isn't fixed. If circumstances change—like a change in income, care arrangements, or the child's needs—the child support amount can be reviewed. Parents can request reassessments through Services Australia.

Private Agreements

While the government provides a structure for determining child support, some parents prefer private agreements. These can be formalised through a child support agreement, which Services Australia can register, giving it the same enforce-ability as a formal child support assessment.

Enforcement

If a parent is not meeting their child support obligations, the paying parent could face enforcement actions, such as wage garnishments or tax return intercepts. Services Australia has various mechanisms to ensure compliance with child support laws.

Types of Child Support Agreements
There are two main types of child support arrangements parents can establish

Administrative Child Support
This is calculated by the CSA using the formula mentioned above. The CSA will manage the collection and distribution of payments between parents.

Private Child Support Agreements
Parents can also choose to make their own arrangements through a private agreement, which must be in writing. While these agreements can offer flexibility, they must still comply with the Child Support Assessment guidelines to ensure that they are in the best interest of the child. Parents can register their private agreement with the CSA for enforcement purposes if necessary.

Enforcing Child Support Payments
If a parent fails to meet their child support obligations, the CSA has various enforcement measures it can employ.

Garnishing wages
The CSA can take payments directly from the parent's salary.

Tax refunds
Any tax refunds owed to the parent can be withheld and redirected to the other parent as child support.

Court orders
The CSA can apply for court orders to enforce payment if necessary.

Important Considerations

Legal Advice
While the CSA provides a straightforward framework for child support calculations, parents should consider seeking legal advice to understand their rights and obligations fully, especially if their situation is complex.

Communication
Open communication between parents is essential for a successful co-parenting arrangement and can help minimise disputes over child support.

Financial Responsibility
It is crucial for both parents to recognise their ongoing financial responsibilities for their children, regardless of their relationship status.

My Thoughts!

Child support in Australia begins as soon as parents separate and is calculated based on the income of both parents, the time each parent spends with the child, and the costs associated with raising the child.

Understanding the processes involved in establishing and maintaining child support is crucial for both parents to ensure the financial stability of their children. By knowing when child support starts and how it is calculated, parents can make informed decisions and arrangements that prioritise the best interests of their children

While I'm not a lawyer, understanding the basics of how child support works in Australia can help parents make informed decisions and ensure their child's best interests are always prioritised.

| 14 |

Other Bills the Ex is Asking to Pay

Navigating financial responsibilities after separation can be complex, especially when it comes to child support and additional expenses. Many parents find themselves in situations where their ex-partner requests contributions toward other bills, such as medical expenses, educational costs, or other shared obligations.

As a family law advocate, I often encounter questions regarding these additional requests and how they can be addressed within the framework of Australian family law.

Here's an overview of what you need to know if your ex is asking you to pay additional bills beyond child support.

Understanding Child Support

In Australia, child support is primarily intended to cover the basic costs of raising a child, such as food, clothing, and housing.
The **Child Support (Assessment) Act 1989** establishes a formula to calculate the financial contributions each parent is required to make,

considering their incomes and the amount of time they spend with the child.

However, child support does not typically encompass all potential expenses. This raises the question what happens when an ex-partner requests additional payments for other bills?

Types of Additional Expenses

Extraordinary Expenses

These may include costs that exceed the usual expenses covered by child support. Common examples include...

- Medical expenses not covered by Medicare or private health insurance, such as dental work, specialist consultations, or therapies.
- Educational costs, including school fees, uniforms, books, extracurricular activities, and childcare.
- Extracurricular activities like sports, music lessons, or camps.

Shared Expenses

Sometimes, parents may share costs associated with joint obligations, such as

- Mortgage payments on a property that is still jointly owned.
- Household bills related to a shared living arrangement, especially if children are still living in the former family home.

Addressing Additional Requests for Payment

When an ex-partner asks for contributions beyond child support, there are several important steps and considerations to keep in mind

Review Your Child Support Agreement

Check the terms of your child support agreement or assessment. In many cases, child support calculations are based solely on basic living expenses and do not include extraordinary expenses unless specified.

Discuss Openly

Open communication with your ex-partner is crucial. Discuss their requests for additional payments and the reasons behind them. Often, a cooperative discussion can lead to an agreement without conflict.

Documentation

Request detailed documentation for any additional expenses claimed.

This should include...

- Invoices or receipts for medical bills or educational costs.
- A clear breakdown of the extraordinary expenses being requested.

Negotiate

If both parties agree on the necessity of these additional costs, you can negotiate how they will be shared. Consider...

- Proportional contributions based on each parent's income.
- Whether the expenses are reasonable and necessary for the child's welfare.

Legal Advice

If negotiations become contentious or you feel overwhelmed by the requests, seeking legal advice is advisable. A family law lawyer can provide guidance on your obligations and rights, helping you navigate the complexities of additional payments.

Family Dispute Resolution

If you cannot reach an agreement through direct communication, consider mediation or family dispute resolution. A mediator can help facilitate the conversation and assist both parties in finding common ground regarding additional expenses.

When Additional Payments Are Enforceable

It's important to understand that if additional payments are agreed upon, they should be documented in writing.

This can be done through

- A private child support agreement, which must comply with the **Child Support Assessment Act**.
- Court orders that outline the specific obligations of each parent regarding extraordinary expenses.

Once agreed upon, these arrangements can be enforced by the Family Court if necessary. Failing to adhere to an agreed payment schedule can lead to legal consequences, including variations in child support assessments or enforcement actions through the Child Support Agency (CSA).

My Thoughts!

When your ex-partner requests additional payments beyond child support, it is essential to approach the situation thoughtfully and collaboratively.

By reviewing your child support agreement, communicating openly, and negotiating fairly, you can address these additional expenses in a way that supports your child's needs while also considering your financial circumstances.

Seeking legal advice can also provide clarity on your obligations and help ensure that any agreements reached are enforceable and in the best interest of your child.

Ultimately, focusing on open communication and cooperation can help reduce conflict and foster a positive co-parenting relationship.

| 15 |

Does Family Law System Protect Me from Violence?

Family violence is a deeply concerning issue that can make navigating the family law system especially challenging. When dealing with the breakdown of a relationship, tensions can be high, and in some cases, one party may feel manipulated or even baited into reacting in ways that could be used against them.

If you're experiencing unusual or provocative behaviour from your ex, it's essential to understand both your legal protections and the steps you can take to protect yourself.

As a family law advocate, I frequently encounter individuals facing these difficult situations. Here's how the Australian family law system can protect you from family violence and what you can do to safeguard your rights if you feel like you're being baited or provoked.

How Does the Family Law System Define Family Violence?

Under the **Family Law Act 1975**, family violence is broadly defined as any violent, threatening, or other behaviour by a person that coerces or controls a family member or causes them to be fearful.

This can include:

Physical violence or threats of violence.

Emotional or psychological abuse, including manipulation, coercion, and gas-lighting.

Economic abuse, such as controlling finances or denying access to money.

Intimidation and harassment, including stalking, constant surveillance, or making veiled threats.

Family violence doesn't only refer to physical harm; it includes any pattern of behaviour that causes you to feel controlled or afraid. This broad definition is crucial because it acknowledges the many forms that family violence can take.

What Legal Protections Are Available?

If you are experiencing family violence, the Australian family law system provides several mechanisms to protect you.

Apprehended Domestic Violence Orders (ADVOs) or Family Violence Orders

If you are being subjected to or threatened with violence, you can apply for a protection order. These are legally enforceable court orders that restrict the abusive party's behaviour.

An ADVO can

- Prevent the person from contacting you, approaching you, or coming near your home or workplace.

- Restrict their behaviour around you, including stopping them from threatening, harassing, or intimidating you.
- If the other party breaches the ADVO, they can face criminal penalties.

Family Court Orders

If you are involved in a parenting dispute, the **Federal Circuit and Family Court of Australia (FCFCOA)** can make orders that protect you and your children from family violence. This might include supervised visitation or limiting the other party's contact with the children if there is a risk of harm.

Court's Focus on Safety

The family law system prioritorizes the best interests of the child, and this includes their safety. If family violence is a factor, the court will take this into account when determining parenting orders. It's important to bring any instances of family violence to the court's attention so that appropriate protections can be put in place.

Independent Children's Lawyer (ICL)

In cases involving serious allegations of family violence, the court may appoint an Independent Children's Lawyer to represent the child's best interests.

The ICL investigates the situation and provides recommendations to the court on parenting arrangements that will protect the child from harm.

What If You Feel Baited or Provoked?

It's not uncommon in high-conflict separations for one party to engage in provocative behaviour—asking unusual questions, making inflammatory statements, or setting up situations that seem designed to get a reaction from you.

This type of behaviour may be intended to provoke you into doing or saying something that could be used against you in court. If you find yourself in this situation, it's critical to protect yourself, both legally and emotionally.

Here's how you can protect yourself if you feel like you're being baited.

Document Everything

If you feel that your ex is trying to provoke you or manipulate the situation, it's essential to document everything.

Keep a record of…

Text messages, emails, and phone conversations that include inflammatory language or baiting behaviour.
Statements made to you during in-person interactions.

Any **threats, harassment**, or attempts to control you.

This documentation will be invaluable if you need to apply for a protection order or present evidence in court. It's important to avoid responding emotionally, even if you're being baited—***keep your communications calm and factual.***

Avoid Reacting Emotionally

While it can be incredibly difficult to remain calm in the face of manipulative behaviour, it's crucial to avoid giving your ex the reaction they're looking for.

If they are trying to provoke you into a heated argument or an outburst, your response could be used against you in family law proceedings, especially if there are disputes over parenting arrangements or custody.

If you receive provocative or inflammatory messages, it's often best to either not respond at all or to respond briefly and factually. Avoid getting drawn into arguments, and don't engage with accusations or baiting questions. The goal is to show the court that you are focused on the well-being of your children and are not contributing to the conflict.

Set Clear Boundaries

Establishing clear boundaries with your ex can help reduce opportunities for them to bait or provoke you. This can include limiting communication to matters directly related to the children or finances, and keeping all conversations via text or email where you can track the tone and content of the exchanges.

Seek Mediation or Legal Advice

If communication with your ex becomes too difficult or volatile, you may want to consider using a third party to mediate conversations. Family Dispute Resolution (FDR) is a form of mediation that can help you work through parenting and financial issues without direct confrontation.

Having a mediator present can reduce the risk of provocative behaviour and create a more structured environment for negotiations.

If the situation continues to escalate, seek legal advice as soon as possible. A family lawyer can help you determine whether you need to apply for a protection order or take other legal steps to safeguard your interests.

Apply for a Family Violence Order If Necessary

If you feel that your ex's behaviour crosses the line into harassment, intimidation, or abuse, don't hesitate to apply for a Family Violence Order. These orders are designed to protect you from further harm and can set strict limits on how the other party interacts with you. Even if the behaviour doesn't involve physical violence, coercive control, harassment, and emotional abuse are forms of family violence that the court takes seriously.

Use Third-Party Drop-Off and Pick-Up Locations for Children

If child exchanges are a flash-point for conflict, consider using a third-party location for pick-up and drop-off. This could be a supervised visitation centre or a neutral location where there is less opportunity for direct confrontation.

Seek Support

Dealing with family violence or manipulative behaviour can be emotionally draining. It's important to have a support system in place, whether that's family, friends, or a therapist who can help you manage the emotional toll.

Staying calm and focused can help protect you from reacting in ways that could be used against you in court.

My Thoughts!

The family law system in Australia provides several protections for individuals experiencing family violence, including protection orders, court orders, and a focus on the safety and well-being of children.

If you feel that your ex is engaging in manipulative or baiting behaviour, it's crucial to protect yourself by documenting the behaviour, avoiding emotional reactions, setting clear boundaries, and seeking legal advice if necessary.

By staying focused on your legal rights and the safety of your family, you can navigate these challenges and protect yourself from further harm.

"I Always Advise...

Document Everything,

***and Focus Keeping Your Communication
Calm and Factual"***

Graham McFarland

| 16 |

How Do Domestic Violence Laws Vary from States?

Australia takes domestic violence very seriously, and laws have been enacted across all states and territories to protect individuals from abuse and violence within the home.

While domestic violence is addressed under the same federal family law principles, domestic violence laws can vary from state to state in terms of their enforcement, processes, and the terminology used.

As a family law advocate, I often help clients navigate these differences, particularly when seeking protection orders or understanding their rights in different jurisdictions.

Here's an overview of how domestic violence laws vary across Australia, including key differences in processes and protections from state to state.

The Core Definition of Domestic Violence
While there are variations between states, the **core definition of domestic violence** is consistent throughout Australia. Domestic violence (or family violence) refers to violent, abusive, or controlling behaviour within a family or intimate relationship.

It can include

Physical violence
Hitting, slapping, pushing, or any form of physical assault.

Emotional or psychological abuse
Manipulation, coercion, gas-lighting, or controlling behaviour.

Verbal abuse
Threats, intimidation, or name-calling.

Financial abuse
Controlling access to money, withholding financial support, or economic coercion.

Stalking or **harassment**
Monitoring movements or communications, making unwanted contact.

Sexual violence
Any non-consensual sexual contact or coercion.

The aim of domestic violence laws is to provide **protection** to victims and ensure that perpetrators are held accountable. However, the way these laws are implemented, and the specifics of certain protections can vary depending on the state or territory.

Domestic Violence Orders Different Names, Similar Purpose

One of the key areas where domestic violence laws differ across states is the name and scope of **protection orders** (also known as restraining orders). These are legal orders issued by a court to protect victims from further harm by limiting the perpetrator's contact or behaviour.

New South Wales

Protection orders are called **Apprehended Domestic Violence Orders (ADVO)**. ADVOs are designed to protect people from violence, harassment, or intimidation by someone with whom they have a domestic relationship.

In NSW, ADVOs can also include provisions to protect children or other family members.

Victoria

In Victoria, these orders are known as **Family Violence Intervention Orders (FVIOs)**. FVIOs are designed to prevent further abuse or violence, and breaches of an FVIO are treated as serious criminal offences.

Victoria also has a **specialist Family Violence Court Division** to handle domestic violence matters more efficiently.

Queensland

In Queensland, domestic violence orders are called **Domestic Violence Protection Orders (DVPOs)**. These orders can be sought by the victim, the police, or an authorised person on behalf of the victim, and they can prevent the perpetrator from contacting or approaching the victim.

Western Australia

WA refers to these orders as **Family Violence Restraining Orders (FVROs)**. A FVRO protects people from violence, intimidation, or threats, and includes a range of conditions designed to keep the victim safe.

South Australia

In South Australia, protection orders are called **Intervention Orders**. These orders are designed to prevent any form of domestic abuse, including emotional or financial abuse, and can apply to a range of relationships, including intimate partners and family members.

Tasmania

In Tasmania, protection orders are known as **Family Violence Orders (FVOs)**. An FVO can be issued by the police or a magistrate to protect individuals from further harm.

Northern Territory

The Northern Territory refers to protection orders as **Domestic Violence Orders (DVOs)**. These can be issued by the police or the court, and the laws in the NT include specific provisions to protect Aboriginal communities, where domestic violence rates are disproportionately high.

Australian Capital Territory

The ACT also uses **Family Violence Orders (FVOs)** to protect victims of domestic abuse. Like other states, these orders aim to limit the perpetrator's contact with the victim and impose strict conditions on their behaviour.

National Recognition of Protection Orders

In the past, a protection order granted in one state would not automatically apply if the victim moved to another state or territory.

However, in 2017, Australia introduced the **National Domestic Violence Order Scheme (NDVOS)**, which ensures that domestic violence protection orders are recognised and enforceable across all states and territories.

Under this scheme, any domestic violence order issued in one state is automatically recognised in all other states and territories.

This means that if you obtain a protection order in New South Wales, it will be valid and enforceable if you move to Queensland, Victoria, or anywhere else in Australia.

The national scheme aims to make it easier for victims to stay protected, even if they move across state borders.

Differences in Police Powers

The way **police** handle domestic violence situations can also vary between states. In some states, the police have broader powers to issue **emergency or temporary protection orders** on the spot without requiring the victim to go through the court process. Here's how this works in some states

New South Wales
NSW police can issue a **Provisional ADVO** immediately if they believe that a person is at risk of domestic violence. This provides immediate protection until a court can make a final decision on the ADVO.

Victoria
In Victoria, police can issue an **Interim FVIO** if they believe someone is at immediate risk. This order is temporary and remains in place until the court can issue a final FVIO.

Queensland
Police in Queensland can issue **Police Protection Notices (PPNs)** in situations where they believe immediate protection is needed. These notices provide temporary protection until the matter can go before a court.

Western Australia
Police in WA can issue an **on-the-spot FVRO** if they believe that a person is at immediate risk of family violence. This gives the victim protection until a court can hear the case.

These emergency orders are particularly important because they allow victims to get immediate protection without needing to go through the court process first.

Differences in Family Violence Court Systems

Some states have specialised court systems or processes designed to handle domestic violence cases more efficiently. For example,

Victoria
Victoria has a **specialised Family Violence Court Division**, which deals exclusively with family violence matters. This division has trained magistrates and staff who specialise in domestic violence cases, and it aims to provide better support to victims and more effective responses to perpetrators.

Western Australia
WA has **specialist family violence courts** in some regions, which are designed to handle domestic violence cases with a greater focus on rehabilitation and ensuring the safety of victims.

Other states are exploring or implementing specialised processes, but not all have dedicated domestic violence courts yet.

Support Services and Legal Aid

While the basic protections provided by domestic violence laws are similar across states, the **support services** available to victims can differ depending on where you live.

Each state has its own network of domestic violence support organisations that help with obtaining protection orders, legal advice, and emergency housing.

Victoria
Organisations like **Safe Steps** and **inTouch** provide a range of services to victims of family violence, including crisis accommodation and legal assistance.

New South Wales

Services such as **Domestic Violence Line** and **Women's Domestic Violence Court Advocacy Service (WDVCAS)** offer support to women seeking protection orders and navigating the court process.

Queensland

The **DVConnect** service offers a 24-hour crisis hot-line and can assist with emergency transport and accommodation for victims of domestic violence.

Each state's Legal Aid services also offer support to victims of domestic violence, helping them apply for protection orders and understand their legal rights.

My Thoughts!

While domestic violence laws in Australia are fundamentally similar across states, there are key differences in the names of protection orders, how police handle emergency situations, and the support services available to victims.

The introduction of the **National Domestic Violence Order Scheme (NDVOS)** has helped streamline protections, ensuring that orders are recognised across state borders, but it's important to understand the specific processes in your state or territory.

If you're facing domestic violence, the law provides several avenues for protection, but seeking help from a legal advocate or domestic violence support service is crucial to navigating the system effectively and ensuring your safety.

"The National Scheme aims
to Make it Easier for Victims to Stay Protected,

Even if They Move Across State Borders".

Graham McFarland

| 17 |

Enhanced Protections for Victim Survivors of DV

Navigating the labyrinth of family law as a family law advocate often means standing at the crossroads where the legal system intersects with deeply personal struggles.

The introduction of new domestic violence laws in New South Wales has brought a renewed focus on protecting victim-survivors, particularly in the context of separation and domestic violence.

These laws are not just legal adjustments; they are a lifeline for individuals trying to reclaim their safety and dignity while navigating complex family dynamics.

Understanding the New Protections

The recent reforms introduced by the NSW Government aim to provide stronger safeguards for victim-survivors of domestic and family violence. Central to these changes is the recognition of the diverse forms of abuse that extend beyond physical violence.

The laws now explicitly acknowledge that coercive control, *"a pattern of controlling and intimidating behaviour"*, is a form of domestic abuse. This is a significant step, as coercive control often remains invisible, yet it is deeply damaging.

For victim-survivors, this means that the legal system is beginning to catch up with the realities of their experiences. It acknowledges that violence is not always visible in bruises and scars; it can be embedded in manipulation, isolation, and control.

By criminalising coercive control, these laws provide a framework to address abuse in its entirety, offering hope for those trapped in its grip.

Impact on Separation and Family Law

In cases of separation, these laws serve as both a shield and a sword. The shield is the enhanced legal protections that allow victim-survivors to step forward with greater confidence that their experiences will be recognised and addressed.

For example, the inclusion of coercive control as a criminal offence means that behaviour's such as financial manipulation, restricting access to children, or monitoring movements can now be presented as evidence of abuse.

The sword, on the other hand, is the ability to use these laws to advocate for fairer outcomes in family law disputes. Separation often brings with it complex negotiations around property settlements, custody arrangements, and parenting plans.

In these contexts, the recognition of coercive control can be pivotal. It enables advocates to argue that certain behaviour's, such as alienation or intimidation, are not just relationship conflicts but abusive tactics that harm both the victim-survivor and any children involved.

In my opinion these new laws also raise challenges. Legal practitioners, advocates, and even judicial officers must be educated to recognise and appropriately handle coercive control.

Without this, the law risks being another well-intentioned reform that fails in its practical application. As an advocate, my role often involves bridging this gap—ensuring that victim-survivors understand their rights while pushing for systemic change to make those rights meaningful.

"The Laws Now Explicitly Recognise That Coercive Control,

Which Is a Pattern of Controlling and Intimidating Behaviour,

Constitutes a Form of Domestic Abuse".

Graham McFarland

The Intersection of Domestic Violence and Parenting

One of the most contentious issues in family law is parenting arrangements in the shadow of domestic violence. The new laws underscore the need to prioritise the safety of children and victim-survivors. This aligns with the principles of the Family Law Act, which places the best interests of the child at the centre of decision-making.

Advocates must now carefully assess how these enhanced protections influence custody and access decisions. For instance, if a parent has been found guilty of coercive control, it becomes easier to argue that their access to children should be supervised or, in extreme cases, restricted.

Yet, this is not without its complexities. Allegations of coercive control may be disputed, and courts must tread carefully to balance protecting children and avoiding false accusations.

The reforms also open doors for victim-survivors to seek intervention orders with expanded protections. These orders can now address behaviour's that fall under the umbrella of coercive control, providing a safer environment for both the victim and their children during and after separation.

This is especially critical in cases where perpetrators use family law processes as a tool of ongoing abuse. I for one can argue that from my exposure to family law, this is a bigger systemic issue that the adjudicators wish to agree with.

Challenges and the Way Forward

While the new laws represent progress, they also highlight areas where the system must improve. One such area is accessibility. Victim-survivors from marginalised communities - such as those with language barriers, disabilities, or who live in rural areas - may still struggle to access the protections these laws promise.

As an advocate, I've often seen how systemic inequities can undermine the best intentions of legislative reform.

Another challenge is ensuring that the legal system does not inadvertently re-traumatize victim-survivors. This requires a trauma-informed approach, where every interaction—from police reports to courtroom proceedings—is handled with sensitivity and understanding.

The adversarial nature of family law proceedings can be particularly difficult for victim-survivors, especially when their abuser uses the system as a weapon of control.

Education and awareness are crucial. Advocates, lawyers, and judicial officers must understand the nuances of coercive control to apply these laws effectively. This also extends to the broader community. The legal system can only do so much; societal attitudes toward domestic violence must evolve alongside legal reforms.

A Step Toward Justice

For victim-survivors of domestic and family violence, the journey to safety and justice will always be fraught with challenges. The new laws introduced in New South Wales are a step in the right direction, offering enhanced protections and a recognition of the realities of abuse.

As a family law advocate, my role is to guide individuals through these legal changes, ensuring that the promises of the law translate into tangible safety and individual empowerment.

Ultimately, these reforms are more than just legislation; they are a commitment to creating a system that prioritises the well-being of those who have endured abuse.

They reflect a growing understanding that justice must be holistic, addressing not just the visible scars but the invisible wounds inflicted by control and intimidation.

In this, we find hope for a future where victim-survivors can not only survive but thrive.

*"In Cases where
Perpetrators Use Family Law Processes
As a Tool of Ongoing Abuse.*

*I For One Can Argue
with My Exposure to Family Law,*

*This Is a Bigger Systemic Issue Than the Courts
Wish to Agree Occurs".*

Graham McFarland

| 18 |

Criminalising Coercive Control

As family law advocates, we often witness the thin line between justice and unintended consequences when new laws are introduced. The criminalisation of coercive control in New South Wales, effective from June 2024, marks a significant shift in addressing the pervasive issue of domestic violence.

It is a necessary evolution in the law, recognising that abuse is not always physical but can manifest through manipulation, isolation, and domination. However, as groundbreaking as these reforms are, they come with complexities that must be approached with caution, particularly in the context of separation and custody disputes.

This chapter aims to explore the nuances of these laws, including the new definitions of coercive control, their intent, and how they may inadvertently ensnare individuals navigating the difficult terrain of separation.

While not providing legal advice, this discussion highlights the importance of understanding the law's implications for all parties involved.

What is Coercive Control?

Coercive control refers to a pattern of behaviour's designed to dominate and intimidate a partner, stripping them of their autonomy and sense of self. The new laws in NSW define coercive control in the context of domestic relationships and categorise it as a criminal offence.

Behaviours that constitute coercive control include, but not limited to...

- Isolating a partner from family and friends.
- Monitoring or controlling their movements and communications.
- Restricting access to financial resources.
- Threatening harm to the partner, children, or pets.
- Stalking or harassment that induces fear.

Under these laws, coercive control is recognised as more than isolated incidents of abuse. It is a pattern of behaviour with cumulative effects, often resulting in psychological trauma.

For victim survivors, this criminalisation is a step toward acknowledging the full spectrum of domestic abuse.

Making Coercive Control a Crime, A Milestone in Law Reform

The NSW Government's decision to criminalise coercive control was driven by the tragic consequences of unrecognised abuse. Research and advocacy revealed that coercive control often precedes physical violence and can escalate to homicide, and in some instances suicide.

By addressing coercive behaviour's before they result in physical harm, these laws aim to save lives.

The law targets abusive patterns in relationships, emphasising that abuse need not be physical to be harmful. For victim-survivors, this provides a critical avenue to seek justice and protection, holding perpetrators accountable for behaviour's that previously fell through the cracks of the legal system.

*"Separation Often Brings Out the
Worst in Relationships,*

*And It Is Not Uncommon For
Allegations of Abuse to Be Used,*

As a Tactical Advantage in Custody Battles".

Graham McFarland

The Challenge of Innocent Missteps

While the intent behind criminalising coercive control is commendable, its application raises significant concerns, particularly for individuals navigating separation and custody arrangements.

In emotionally charged situations, where accusations and counter-accusations are common, the risk of innocent individuals being labelled as perpetrators is real. This is something that drives many a family law advocate.

Consider a parent who checks in frequently on their children after separation, ensuring their safety during access visits. While their actions may stem from genuine concern, an ex-partner often interprets this as monitoring or controlling behaviour.

Similarly, disputes over financial arrangements during separation—common and often contentious—could be framed as financial abuse if misinterpreted.

The new laws place a heavy burden on interpreting intent. In cases of separation, where emotions are heightened, misunderstandings or retaliatory claims can lead to accusations of coercive control.

Innocent actions may be scrutinised through the lens of the law, especially in contentious separations where bitterness clouds judgement.

The Risk of Weaponisation

One of the most troubling aspects of these reforms is the potential for weaponisation in family law disputes. Separation often brings out the worst in relationships, and it is not uncommon for allegations of abuse to be used as a tactical advantage in custody battles.

With the criminalisation of coercive control, the stakes are higher than ever.

For example, a parent seeking greater access to their children might allege coercive control by their ex-partner, knowing that such allegations could influence court decisions. While the law requires evidence of a pattern of behaviour, the mere accusation can have devastating consequences for the accused. They may face criminal investigations, damage to their reputation, and limited access to their children—all before guilt is determined.

This risk is real and dominates a high proportion of cases I personally have experienced over the decades. In most of these cases, counterclaiming against this weaponisation, results in vilification of the real innocent party, and their own support network.

*"Society Often Scoffs at the Thought that
Weaponisation is even possible,*

and When I Talk About Weaponizing this way,

*it is the First Step Towards me Being Disenfranchised
From the Conversation".*

Graham McFarland

A Cautious Approach

As advocates, it is crucial to approach these laws with caution. While supporting victim survivors is paramount, we must also recognise the potential for misuse and unintended harm. The criminalisation of coercive control is a tool for justice, but like any tool, its effectiveness depends on its application.

Education is vital. Both the public and professionals within the legal system must understand the nuances of coercive control to prevent misuse of the law. Judicial officers, police, and family law practitioners need training to differentiate between genuine patterns of abuse and situational behaviour's arising from separation.

It is also essential for accused individuals to seek legal advice and representation promptly. The legal system offers mechanisms to contest allegations, but navigating these processes requires expertise. As advocates, we must guide individuals to appropriate legal resources, ensuring they understand their rights and responsibilities under these new laws.

Balancing Protection and Fairness

The criminalisation of coercive control is a significant step forward in protecting victim survivors of domestic violence. It acknowledges the profound harm caused by psychological and emotional abuse, offering a pathway to justice that was previously unavailable.

However, it is not without risks. Innocent individuals, particularly those navigating the complexities of separation and custody, may find themselves entangled in accusations of coercive control.

As these laws are implemented, the legal system must strike a balance between protecting victim-survivors and safeguarding against misuse. This requires careful application of the law, supported by education, training, and robust mechanisms for investigating allegations.

For advocates, our role is to support individuals on both sides of this divide, ensuring that justice is both fair and compassionate.

Final Thoughts

The criminalisation of coercive control in NSW reflects a growing recognition of the complexities of domestic violence. While it offers hope for victim-survivors, it also serves as a cautionary tale about the potential for unintended consequences.

As we move forward, the challenge will be to harness the power of these laws to protect those in need while ensuring that they are not misused to harm the innocent.

This is not legal advice, but a call for awareness and caution. The introduction of these laws is a turning point in family law, and understanding their implications is essential for anyone navigating this landscape.

*"Innocent Actions May be Scrutinised
Through the Lens of the Law,*

*Especially in Contentious Separations
Where Bitterness Clouds Judgement".*

Graham McFarland

| 19 |

How is Property and Assets Divided?

When couples go through a divorce or separation, one of the most pressing concerns is how property and assets will be divided.

In Australia, the law provides a fair and equitable process for dividing marital property, but this doesn't necessarily mean a 50/50 split.

Instead, the court considers a range of factors to ensure that the division of property is fair to both parties. As a family law advocate, I've often guided individuals through understanding how assets, including superannuation, are divided during a divorce or separation.

Here's an overview of the process and some important points to consider.

Property Division in Australia

In Australia, property settlements after divorce or separation are governed by the **Family Law Act 1975**. This includes not only married couples but also defacto relationships, provided certain criteria are met.

The term "property" covers all types of assets owned by the couple, such as the family home, investment properties, cars, bank accounts, shares, businesses, and personal belongings.

The division of property is typically done through either **negotiation** (with or without the help of lawyers), **mediation**, or by applying to the **Federal Circuit and Family Court of Australia (FCFCOA)** for property orders if an agreement cannot be reached.

The Four-Step Process

The court uses a well-established **four-step process** to determine how property should be divided between separating parties. This process considers each person's contribution to the relationship as well as their future needs.

1. Identify the Assets and Liabilities

The first step is to create a detailed list of all the assets and liabilities of both parties. This includes everything of value, such as the family home, cars, savings, debts, and even superannuation.

Both parties are required to make a full and frank disclosure of their financial situation, which means they must declare all assets, liabilities, and income. Failure to disclose assets can lead to penalties or court orders being overturned later.

2. Assess Contributions

Next, the court assesses each party's contributions to the relationship, both financial and non-financial. Financial contributions can include income earned, savings brought into the relationship, or property purchased during the marriage.

Non-financial contributions include homemaking, raising children, and other unpaid work that benefits the family.

Both initial contributions (before the relationship) and ongoing contributions throughout the marriage or de facto relationship are considered. For example, if one partner was the primary earner while the other took care of the children and household, these roles are considered equally important.

3. Assess Future Needs

The court then looks at the future needs of both parties.

This includes factors such as:

- The age and health of each party.
- Whether one party has primary care of children.
- The income-earning capacity of each party.
- Whether either party will need ongoing financial support (spousal maintenance).

For example, if one party is the primary caregiver for young children and has a lower earning capacity, they may be entitled to a larger share of the property to ensure their financial security going forward.

4. Arriving at a Just and Equitable Outcome

The court ensures that the division of property is just and equitable. This doesn't mean that property will be split equally down the middle; rather, it will be divided in a way that is fair, considering the contributions of each party and their future needs.

If the matter goes to court, the judge will make orders based on the specific circumstances of the case. Most couples prefer to reach an agreement outside of court through negotiation or mediation, which can save time, money, and stress.

Superannuation and Divorce

In Australia, superannuation is considered property and is treated similarly to other assets during divorce or separation. This means it can be divided between the parties, even though it's not usually accessible until retirement. The division of superannuation is known as superannuation splitting.

How Superannuation Splitting Works

Identify Superannuation Interests
The first step is to determine the value of each party's superannuation. This is done by contacting the superannuation fund and obtaining a valuation.

Superannuation can include both accumulation funds (where contributions grow over time) and defined benefit schemes (which provide specific retirement benefits based on salary and years of service).

Splitting the Superannuation
Superannuation splitting allows part of one party's superannuation to be transferred to the other party. This is done through a superannuation agreement or a court order. The transferred amount is placed into the recipient's superannuation fund and remains there until they are eligible to access it, usually upon retirement.

It's important to note that superannuation splitting does not mean the money is immediately accessible. The superannuation stays within the fund until the conditions for release (like retirement) are met.

Reaching an Agreement or Court Orders

You can agree on how superannuation will be split as part of a property settlement agreement. If you and your ex-partner agree, you can submit consent orders to the court for approval. If no agreement is reached, the court can make orders dividing the superannuation, just like other assets.

While superannuation splitting is a common part of property division, some people choose to offset superannuation against other assets. For example, one partner might keep their superannuation in exchange for giving the other party a larger share of other property, such as the family home.

What About Debts?

It's important to understand that liabilities, such as mortgages, credit card debts, and personal loans, are also part of the property settlement. The court will consider who is responsible for these debts and how they should be divided between the parties.

Even if a debt is in one person's name, it may be considered a joint responsibility if it was used to benefit the relationship (e.g., a loan used to buy a family car or renovate the home).

Reaching an Agreement Out of Court

While the court process is available for property settlements, it's often preferable to resolve these matters out of court through negotiation or Family Dispute Resolution (FDR). Couples who can reach an agreement can have their settlement formalised by the court through consent orders.

It's important to seek legal advice before finalising any property settlement, as the agreement must be just and equitable. Once a court has approved a consent order, it is legally binding, and both parties must adhere to its terms.

Time Limits for Property Settlements

For married couples, you must apply for property settlement within 12 months of the divorce being finalized. For de facto couples, you have two years from the date of separation to apply.

After these time limits, you need special permission from the court to file for a property settlement.

My Thoughts!

In Australia, property and assets are divided based on a fair and equitable approach, rather than an automatic 50/50 split. The court considers each party's contributions to the relationship, as well as their future needs, to reach a just outcome.

Superannuation, which is often one of the largest assets for couples, is also included in the division process and can be split between the parties.

Whether you resolve your property settlement through negotiation, mediation, or court, seeking legal advice is essential to ensure your rights are protected and that the settlement is fair.

| 20 |

What Happens with Undeclared Assets?

One of the most frustrating situations during a separation or divorce can be discovering that your ex is hiding assets or failing to disclose their full financial situation.

In Australia, the law requires both parties in a separation to make a full and frank disclosure of all their assets, liabilities, and financial resources. Failing to do so can have serious legal consequences.

As a family law advocate, I often guide clients through the process of dealing with undeclared assets and ensuring that the property settlement is fair and transparent.

Here's what happens when undeclared assets come to light and how you can address the issue.

The Legal Requirement for Full and Frank Disclosure

Under Australian family law, both parties to a divorce or separation are legally required to provide full and frank disclosure of all their financial circumstances. This includes…

All **assets** (such as property, shares, savings, and businesses).
All **liabilities** (such as mortgages, loans, and debts).
Any **other** financial resources, including superannuation or trusts.

This requirement is part of ensuring that any property settlement or financial order is based on an accurate understanding of the couple's financial situation. Full disclosure is essential because it helps the court (or both parties, if negotiating out of court) determine a just and equitable division of assets.

What Happens If Assets Are Not Disclosed?

If one party fails to disclose assets, it can have serious consequences, both legally and financially. Here are some potential outcomes if undeclared assets are discovered

Set Aside Orders

If the court finds out that one party has failed to disclose assets or has intentionally hidden them, it has the power to set aside any previous financial agreements or orders that were based on incomplete information.

This means that even if a financial settlement has already been made, it could be reopened and revised to reflect the true financial situation.

Penalties for Non-Disclosure

Failing to disclose assets or attempting to hide them from the court is seen as a serious breach of legal duty. The court can impose penalties on the person who did not disclose their assets, which could include fines or being ordered to pay the other party's legal costs.

Adverse Inferences

The court may also make adverse inferences against the party hiding assets. This means that the court could assume that the hidden assets were of substantial value and adjust the property settlement in favour of the other party.

In some cases, this could result in the other party receiving a larger share of the disclosed assets.

Contempt of Court

If the court determines that a party has deliberately provided false information or withheld financial details, they could be found in contempt of court. This is a serious offence that can lead to sanctions, including financial penalties or, in extreme cases, imprisonment.

How to Handle Undeclared Assets

If you know that your ex is hiding assets or failing to disclose their full financial situation, it's crucial to take steps to protect your rights and ensure a fair settlement. Here's how to handle the situation

Gather Evidence

Before taking any action, it's important to gather as much evidence as possible about the undeclared assets. This could include…

- Bank statements, emails, or documents that show your ex's ownership of property, shares, or other assets.
- Information about hidden bank accounts, offshore investments, or trusts.
- Business records or financial statements that show discrepancies between declared income and actual financial circumstances.

If you have reason to believe that your ex is hiding assets, but you don't have access to the full details, you may need to enlist professional help (such as a forensic accountant) to investigate further.

Request Full Disclosure

In family law cases, both parties must submit a financial statement as part of the property settlement process. If you suspect that your ex is not disclosing all of their assets, you can request that they provide more detailed information. You have the right to ask for full disclosure of any financial documents, including tax returns, bank statements, and property deeds.

If your ex continues to withhold information, you can ask the court to intervene by issuing an order for discovery. This is a formal process where the court requires the other party to produce specific documents or information.

File an Application in Court

If your ex is refusing to disclose assets, or if you have concrete evidence of hidden assets, you can file an application with the Federal Circuit and Family Court of Australia (FCFCOA). The court can order your ex to provide full disclosure of all assets and can penalise them if they fail to comply.

Additionally, if you discover the undeclared assets after a financial settlement has been made, you may be able to apply to the court to set aside the original settlement and have the matter reconsidered considering the new information.

Seek Legal Advice

Dealing with hidden or undeclared assets can be legally complex. It's essential to seek advice from a family lawyer who has experience in property settlements and non-disclosure issues. They can guide you on the best approach to uncovering hidden assets and ensuring that you receive a fair share of the property.

Undeclared Assets and Property Settlements

When it comes to property settlements, the court's primary goal is to ensure that the division of assets is just and equitable. If one party is hiding assets, it undermines this goal and can lead to an unfair settlement.

To address this, the court has wide-ranging powers to ensure fairness. This can include redistributing the property, awarding a greater share to the honest party, or ordering that previously undisclosed asset be included in the property pool.

In cases where the other party's financial dishonesty comes to light after the settlement has been finalised, the court can revisit the case if it believes that there has been a miscarriage of justice due to fraud, non-disclosure, or mistake.

This means that even if your property settlement is already finalised, you may still be able to challenge it if you discover that assets were hidden.

Protecting Your Rights in Property Settlements

If you're concerned that your ex is hiding assets, here are some key steps to protect your rights

Ensure full disclosure
Make sure that all financial documents are disclosed before agreeing to any property settlement.

Get legal advice

Having a lawyer who understands property settlements and non-disclosure issues can help you navigate the process.

Use discovery tools

If your ex refuses to provide full disclosure, your lawyer can request discovery through the court to obtain the necessary documents.

Investigate suspicious activity

If you notice any red flags—such as significant withdrawals, unaccounted for income, or secretive behaviour—don't hesitate to investigate it further with the help of a legal professional or forensic accountant.

My Thoughts!

Undeclared or hidden assets can complicate the process of reaching a fair property settlement, but Australian family law has mechanisms in place to deal with these situations. If you believe your ex is hiding assets, it's essential to gather evidence, request full disclosure, and seek legal advice.

The court takes non-disclosure seriously and can impose penalties on parties who fail to provide an honest account of their financial situation.

By taking the proper steps, you can protect your rights and ensure that you receive a fair and equitable share of the property.

*"The Court Takes
Non-Disclosure Seriously,*

And ...

*Can Impose Penalties on Parties
Who Fail to Provide an Honest Account,*

*Of Their
Financial Situation".*

Graham McFarland

| 21 |

Can I Relocate My Child After a Separation?

Relocating with your child after a separation or divorce is one of the more complex and emotionally charged issues in family law.

As a family law advocate, I often encounter questions from parents wondering whether they are legally allowed to move with their child—whether it's to another city, state, or even country—after their relationship ends.

The simple answer is...
"Yes, you can relocate, but it's not that straightforward".

The decision to move with a child requires careful consideration of legal obligations, the other parent's rights, and most importantly, what is in the best interests of the child.

Here's what you need to know about relocating your child after a separation or divorce in Australia.

The Best Interests of the Child

In Australian family law, any decision that affects a child must always prioritise the **best interests of the child**. This is the primary consideration under the **Family Law Act 1975**.

When it comes to relocation, the court (or both parents, if they can agree) must evaluate whether the move is in the child's best interests, considering...

- The child's need to maintain a meaningful relationship with both parents.
- The emotional and social impact of the move on the child.
- The practicalities of maintaining ongoing contact with the non-relocating parent.

These factors play a crucial role in whether relocation is permitted, as the law aims to ensure that the child continues to have strong and supportive relationships with both parents after separation.

Do You Need Permission to Relocate?

Whether you need permission to relocate with your child depends on the circumstances.

When Both Parents Agree

If both parents agree on the relocation, the process is relatively straightforward. It's always advisable to put the agreement in writing and formalize it through consent orders in the Federal Circuit and Family Court of Australia (FCFCOA).

This makes the agreement legally binding and enforceable, reducing the likelihood of future disputes.

When Parents Disagree

If the other parent opposes the relocation, you **cannot move with the child without either the other parent's consent or a court order**.

Relocating without permission can lead to serious legal consequences, including being ordered to return the child to the previous location and potentially facing allegations of breaching parenting orders.

If an agreement cannot be reached between you and the other parent regarding relocation, it will be necessary to seek permission from the court. The court will evaluate the circumstances and make a decision based on the best interests of the child.

Court Considerations for Relocation

If relocation becomes a court matter, the judge will consider a variety of factors before granting or denying the request to move with the child.

These include…

Reasons for the Relocation

The court will also look at the relocating parent's reasons for wanting to move. Legitimate reasons for relocation might include

- A **job opportunity** that provides financial stability.
- Moving closer to **extended family** who can provide support.
- The need to escape **family violence** or create a safer environment for the child.

The Child's Relationship with Both Parents

The court will evaluate how the relocation impacts the child's relationship with the non-relocating parent. The law typically presumes that it is beneficial for children to maintain a close and meaningful relationship with both parents.

If the relocation would significantly restrict or harm that relationship, the court may be less inclined to approve the move.

Practicality of Contact Arrangements

The court will consider whether there are realistic and practical ways to maintain regular contact between the child and the non-relocating parent. For example, the relocating parent may need to demonstrate how they will facilitate regular visits or maintain communication through phone calls, video chats, or extended holiday visits.

However, if the relocation is seen as an attempt to reduce the other parent's involvement in the child's life, the court may be less inclined to approve the move.

Impact on the Child

The court will assess how the relocation affects the child's emotions, education, friendships, and overall stability. The preferences of older children may be taken into account, though they are only one factor in the decision.

Alternatives to Relocation

The court may consider whether there are viable alternatives to relocation that would allow the relocating parent to achieve their goals (e.g job opportunities or support from extended family) without moving the child far from the other parent.

What Happens if You Relocate Without Permission?

Relocating with a child without the other parent's consent or a court order is a serious matter and can have significant legal consequences.

If you move without permission…

- The other parent may apply to the court for **recovery orders** to have the child returned.
- The court may view your actions unfavourably in future custody or parenting disputes, as it may be seen as attempting to undermine the child's relationship with the other parent.
- In extreme cases, relocating without permission could lead to accusations of **child abduction**, especially if the move is international.

International Relocation

Relocating internationally with a child after separation is particularly complicated. In most cases, you will need the other parent's **written consent** or a **court order** to move overseas with your child.

The court is likely to scrutinize international relocations even more closely than domestic moves, as the distance involved can make it extremely difficult for the child to maintain regular contact with the non-relocating parent.

The court will consider factors such as…

- Whether the child will have sufficient opportunities to visit the non-relocating parent.
- Whether the child will be able to maintain regular communication with the other parent.
- The stability and safety of the proposed new environment.

Before an international move, seek legal advice and obtain proper permissions to avoid serious legal consequences under the **Hague Convention on International Child Abduction**.

Applying to the Court for Relocation

If you need to relocate and the other parent does not consent, you will need to apply to the **FCFCOA** for permission.

The court process involves...

- Filing an application for a relocation order, detailing your reasons for wanting to relocate.
- Attending hearings where both parties present their arguments, allowing the court to determine what serves the child's best interests.
- Providing evidence that demonstrates how the move will benefit the child and how you plan to maintain the child's relationship with the other parent.

Resolving Relocation Disputes

While the court process is an option for resolving relocation disputes, it's often preferable for parents to try to reach an agreement without going to court. Mediation or **Family Dispute Resolution (FDR)** can help facilitate discussions and encourage both parties to find a solution that works for everyone, particularly the child.

Mediation allows parents to explore alternative arrangements, such as...

- Adjusting the existing parenting plan to accommodate the move.
- Setting up long-distance parenting plans that allow for extended visits during school holidays.

- Arranging for virtual communication to supplement face-to-face visits.

My Thoughts!

Relocating with your child after separation or divorce requires either the other parent's consent or court approval. The primary focus is on the child's best interests, including maintaining relationships with both parents.

If you're planning to relocate, get legal advice early and understand your obligations and the other parent's rights. Aim for a cooperative solution to protect your child's well-being and family relationships.

*"It's Always Advisable to Put The Agreement
In Writing and Formalise It,*

*Through Consent Orders
In The Court".*

Graham McFarland

| 22 |

We Got Married, How Does This Change Things?

Marriage is a significant legal and personal commitment, and in Australia, it brings certain legal changes that can impact your rights and responsibilities, especially in the context of family law.

As a family law advocate, I often help couples understand how marriage affects matters like property, finances, and parental responsibilities.

While defacto couples also have many similar rights, marriage formalises your relationship in a way that can influence key areas of your life.

Here's an overview of how getting married changes things in terms of family law.

Legal Recognition of Your Relationship

The most immediate change after getting married is that your relationship is now legally recognised as a **marriage** under the **Marriage Act 1961**. This distinction provides automatic legal rights and obligations that may not have been as clear or automatic if you were in a defacto relationship. For example…

You are now presumed to be each other's **next of kin**, which can affect medical decisions or inheritance rights.

Your marriage is recognised by the government and other institutions for legal and financial purposes.

While defacto couples can gain many of these rights after living together for a certain period (usually two years) or having a child together, marriage formalises these rights from the moment you legally wed.

Property and Financial Arrangements

One of the most significant areas where marriage affects family law is in the division of property and assets.

Property Settlement

When a marriage ends, the **Family Law Act 1975** oversees how property is divided between spouses. The law recognises that both partners have contributed to the marriage in different ways, whether financially or non-financially (like homemaking or raising children). These contributions are considered during property settlement decisions.

Marriage does not automatically mean an equal 50/50 split, but it does mean that the court will consider what is just and equitable based on factors such as financial contributions, non-financial contributions, and future needs.

If you were already in a defacto relationship, your property rights might not change significantly with marriage, as Australian law already provides similar protections for defacto couples when it comes to property settlement.

Financial Responsibilities

Once married, both spouses are considered legally responsible for joint financial decisions. This includes the ability to enter financial contracts together and responsibilities for shared debts, regardless of whose name is on the loan or contract.

Any property acquired during the marriage, whether in one partner's name or both, can be subject to division upon separation.

Superannuation

Superannuation is considered part of the property pool in family law, and this applies to both married and de facto couples. However, being married can make it easier to claim your spouse's superannuation upon their death or through a property settlement.

Spousal Maintenance

After marriage, if a separation occurs, one party may be entitled to **spousal maintenance** (commonly referred to as "alimony" in some countries). This legal obligation requires one spouse to financially support the other if they cannot meet their own reasonable expenses post-separation.

The entitlement to spousal maintenance is based on
- The financial needs of the requesting spouse.
- The ability of the other spouse to provide support.

This is different from **child support**, which is specifically for the child's needs, and is often a key consideration after divorce or separation for married couples, especially if one spouse sacrificed their career for the marriage.

Just to note, that in Australia it is viewed that both parents are capable to work and earn a living. It is therefore uncommon to apply for spousal maintenance, unless there are extraordinary circumstances.

Parental Responsibility and Child Custody

Marriage doesn't automatically change your rights or obligations as parents if you already have children together, but it does formalise them in certain ways.

Under the **Family Law Act**, both parents, whether married or defacto, have equal rights and responsibilities when it comes to decisions about their children. This concept is known as **parental responsibility**.

However, being married can affect other aspects of parenthood

Automatic Parental Responsibility
If a child is born to a married couple, both parents automatically share equal parental responsibility. This also applies to defacto couples, but marriage can make certain legal aspects (such as naming both parents on birth certificates) more straightforward.

Decision-Making
Married couples are generally presumed to share in the decision-making about the child's welfare, education, and health unless a court order says otherwise.

Wills and Inheritance
Marriage also has significant implications when it comes to **wills** and **inheritance**. Here's how getting married affects these areas

Automatic Revocation of a Will

In most Australian states, getting married automatically **revokes** any existing will, unless the will was made in contemplation of the marriage. If you don't create a new will after marriage, your estate will be distributed according to intestacy laws, which may not align with your wishes.

Inheritance Rights

As a spouse, you are automatically entitled to a share of your partner's estate under intestacy laws if they die without a valid will. In most cases, the surviving spouse will receive most of the estate.

My Thoughts!

In summary, marriage is not only a deeply personal commitment but also a legal shift that brings new rights and responsibilities under Australian family law. As a family law advocate, I've seen how these changes can impact couples' lives, from property and financial arrangements to spousal maintenance, parental responsibilities, and inheritance rights.

While this chapter provides a foundational understanding of how marriage can change things legally,

> *"I cannot stress enough the importance of seeking professional legal advice for your unique situation".*

Every relationship and family dynamic are different, and laws can be complex and evolving. Speaking with a qualified family lawyer can help clarify your specific rights and obligations, ensuring that you make informed decisions and protect your future.

Marriage introduces new legal frameworks that may not have been present or as clear in a de facto relationship, so understanding these changes with guidance from legal professionals can empower you to approach your married life with confidence and security.

"Family Law Act 1975.

*The Law Assumes
that Both Parties have Contributed to the Marriage,*

Be it Financially or Non-Financially"...

Graham McFarland

| 23 |

When and How Can You Get Divorced in Australia?

As a family law advocate, I often help people understand the steps involved in getting divorced in Australia. Divorce can be an emotional and stressful process, but Australian law has a clear framework for when you can apply for divorce and how to go about it.

In this opinion piece, I'll break down the key requirements and steps for obtaining a divorce in Australia.

When Can You Get Divorced in Australia?
To get divorced in Australia, there are several legal requirements that must be met. The most important of these is that the marriage must have **irretrievably broken down**.

Here's a closer look at the requirements

12-Month Separation Period
Under Australian law, you and your spouse must have been **separated for at least 12 months** before you can apply for a divorce. This separation period is the key factor in showing that the marriage has irretrievably broken down.

The separation can be physical (living apart) or "separation under one roof," where you remain in the same home but lead separate lives. If you are separated under one roof, you'll need to provide additional evidence of the separation.

It's important to note that if you reconcile for up to **three months** during the separation period and then separate again, this does not reset the 12-month clock. However, if you reconcile for more than three months, the separation period will restart.

Jurisdictional Requirements

You can apply for a divorce in Australia if you or your spouse meet one of the following conditions

- You are an Australian citizen.
- You regard Australia as your permanent home.
- You ordinarily live in Australia and have done so for at least **12 months** before filing for divorce.

This means that even if you were married overseas, you can still get divorced in Australia if you meet the residency requirements.

How Do You Get Divorced in Australia?

Now that we've covered when you can get divorced, let's go through the steps involved in the process. The process is relatively straightforward, but it's important to follow each step carefully to avoid delays or complications.

Filing the Application for Divorce

To start the divorce process, you will need to file an Application for Divorce with the Federal Circuit and Family Court of Australia

(FCFCOA). You can file the application online via the Commonwealth Courts Portal. There are two types of applications…

Sole Application
You can apply for a divorce on your own if your spouse does not agree to the divorce or you are not in contact with them.

Joint Application
You and your spouse can apply for divorce together, which can simplify the process and avoid the need for a court hearing.

If you file a sole application, you will need to serve the divorce papers on your spouse, and they must be given at least 28 days' notice before the hearing (or 42 days if they live overseas).

Court Hearing
If you file a **joint application**, you typically won't need to attend a court hearing, and the divorce will be processed administratively. However, if you file a **sole application** and you have children under 18, you may be required to attend a short court hearing. The court will ensure that proper arrangements have been made for the care and welfare of the children before granting the divorce. If no children are involved, the hearing may not be required.

The court hearing is generally a straightforward process, and if everything is in order, the divorce will be granted. It's important to note that the court does not deal with issues like property settlement or parenting arrangements as part of the divorce process, those matters are handled separately.

Divorce Order
Once the court grants the divorce, it becomes final **one month and one day** after the divorce is granted. At this point, the court will issue a **Divorce Order**, which legally ends the marriage.

If you need a copy of the Divorce Order (for example, to remarry or for legal purposes), you can download it from the Commonwealth Courts Portal.

Key Considerations

Property Settlements and Parenting Arrangements
Divorce does not resolve issues related to property division or child custody. If you have property or children with your spouse, these matters need to be dealt with separately. The law encourages separating couples to reach agreements through negotiation or mediation before applying to the court for orders.

You have **12 months** from the date the divorce is finalised to apply for a property settlement or spousal maintenance. After that, you need special permission from the court to file.

Marriage Certificate
To apply for a divorce, you will need a copy of your **marriage certificate**. If you were married overseas, you may need to have your marriage certificate translated into English and certified.

Costs
There is a filing fee for applying for divorce, which as of 2024 is **$1,060**. If you are experiencing financial hardship, you may be eligible for a reduced fee or fee waiver.

Legal Advice
While you can apply for divorce without a lawyer, it's a good idea to seek legal advice, especially if there are disputes over children or property. A lawyer can help you understand your rights and ensure the process goes smoothly.

Alternatives to Divorce

Sometimes couples may wish to live separately but not divorce. In these cases, a **legal separation** or **separation under one roof** may be an option, allowing both parties to remain legally married while living apart.

If you're unsure about whether divorce is the right option for you, seeking legal advice can help you understand your options and make an informed decision.

My Thoughts!

In Australia, you can apply for a divorce after being separated for at least 12 months and meeting the necessary residency requirements.

The divorce process itself is straightforward, especially if both parties agree and file a joint application. While divorce legally ends the marriage, it doesn't resolve issues related to property or parenting, which need to be dealt with separately.

If you are considering divorce, seeking legal advice and understanding the steps involved can help ensure a smooth and efficient process.

"Australia has a No-Fault Divorce System,

*Meaning that Neither Party Needs to Prove
that the Other Was
at Fault for the Breakdown of the Marriage.*

*The Only Requirement is
that the Marriage has Irretrievably Broken Down,*

by the 12-month Separation Period".

Graham McFarland

| 24 |

Getting Divorced After Being Married Overseas.

As a family law advocate, I often receive questions from individuals who were married overseas but now reside in Australia and wish to divorce. The good news is that it is possible to get divorced in Australia, even if your marriage took place in another country.

However, there are some important requirements and considerations to be aware of.

Can You Get Divorced in Australia?
The short answer is yes. Australian family law allows you to apply for a divorce even if you were married in another country, if certain criteria are met.

According to the **Family Law Act 1975**, your overseas marriage must be legally recognized in Australia, and you need to meet specific residency or citizenship requirements.

You can apply for divorce in Australia if you

- **Are an Australian citizen** (by birth, descent, or by grant of citizenship),

- **Live in Australia** and regard it as your permanent home, or
- Have been **ordinarily living in Australia for at least 12 months** before applying for the divorce.
-

Is Your Overseas Marriage Recognised in Australia?

For the divorce to proceed, your marriage must be legally recognised in Australia. Generally, Australia recognises overseas marriages as long as they comply with the laws of the country where the marriage took place.

This includes meeting basic requirements, such as..

- You were both of legal age to marry,
- You both freely consented to the marriage,
- The marriage was properly solemnised under local laws.

If your overseas marriage does not meet these criteria (for example, if it involves forced or underage marriage), it might not be recognised in Australia.

To prove your marriage, you will need to provide a marriage certificate from the country where the marriage was solemnised. If this certificate is not in English, you'll need to provide an officially translated version.

What Else Should You Know About Getting Divorced in Australia?

12-Month Separation Requirement

In Australia, you must be separated from your spouse for at least 12 months before applying for a divorce. This separation period can occur while living under the same roof, but you'll need to provide evidence that the relationship has broken down.

No-Fault Divorce
Australia operates under a "no-fault" divorce system. This means the only requirement is that the marriage has irretrievably broken down, demonstrated by the 12-month separation. You do not need to prove wrongdoing or assign blame.

Other Legal Issues
While divorce ends the legal marriage, it doesn't resolve other issues like property settlement or child custody. These matters are dealt with separately under family law, and it's important to seek legal advice or advocacy support when dealing with these complexities.

Common Concerns

What If My Spouse Is Overseas?
You can still apply for a divorce if your spouse lives overseas. However, you will need to serve divorce papers on them, and this can sometimes be challenging. Australia's family law courts provide guidance on how to serve documents internationally, but the process may take longer depending on the country involved.

What If I Can't Locate My Spouse?
If you can't find your spouse, you can apply to the court for "substituted service" or "dispensation of service," where alternative methods of serving documents can be approved.

Will My Overseas Divorce Be Recognised Elsewhere?
Divorce orders issued in Australia are typically acknowledged by most countries. However, if international recognition is crucial, it

is advisable to consult with the relevant authorities in your spouse's country.

My Thoughts!

Getting divorced in Australia after being married overseas is generally straightforward, provided you meet the residency and separation requirements, and your overseas marriage is legally recognised.

While the process can involve additional steps—like providing translated documents or serving papers overseas—it's fully achievable.

By understanding the legal framework, you can take steps toward finalising your divorce with confidence.

| 25 |

Traveling with Children After Separation.

When travelling with children, without the accompaniment of one or both parents requires careful preparation to address legal requirements and ensure the emotional well-being of the child.

As a family law advocate, I offer the following comprehensive guidance to help you navigate this process effectively.

Legal Considerations

Consent Documentation

When a child travels with only one parent or a non-parent guardian, it's crucial to carry a Child Travel Consent Form. This notarised document, signed by the non-travelling parent(s) or legal guardians, grants permission for the child to travel and typically includes

- The child's full name and date of birth.
- Details of the accompanying adult(s).
- Travel itinerary, including destinations and dates.
- Contact information for the non-travelling parent(s).

This form serves as proof of consent and can prevent potential legal issues during travel.

Passport Requirements

All children, regardless of age, must possess their own passport for international travel. In Australia, obtaining a child's passport requires the consent of all individuals with parental responsibility.

If consent is not obtainable, a court order permitting the child to have a passport or travel internationally may be necessary.

Airline Policies

Airlines have specific protocols for minors traveling without both parents. Some may require additional documentation or have policies regarding unaccompanied minors.

It's essential to verify these requirements with the airline prior to travel to ensure compliance.

Destination Country Regulations

Different countries have varying entry requirements for minors travelling without both parents. Some may demand additional documentation, such as proof of custody or notarised consent letters.

Contact the embassy or consulate of the destination country to confirm specific requirements.

Family Law Watch-list

In situations where there is concern about a child being taken overseas without appropriate consent, a parent can apply to have the child's name placed on the Family Law Watch list.

This action can prevent the child from leaving Australia without proper authorisation.

Emotional Considerations

Preparation and Communication
Discuss the travel plans with your child in advance to alleviate anxiety. Explain the purpose of the trip, the itinerary, and address any concerns they may have.

Familiar Items
Encourage your child to bring along familiar items, such as a favourite toy or blanket, to provide comfort during the journey.

Maintain Routine
As much as possible, keep to your child's regular routines, including meal times and sleep schedules, to provide a sense of normalcy.

Stay Connected
Arrange regular communication with the non-travelling parent to maintain the child's sense of security and family connection.

Emotional Support
Be attentive to your child's emotional needs throughout the trip. Encourage them to express their feelings and provide reassurance as needed.

Practical Tips

Medical Considerations
Carry a Child Medical Consent form, which authorises the accompanying adult to make medical decisions on behalf of the child if necessary.

This document should include The child's health information, authorised medical treatments, emergency contact details.

Health Precautions

Ensure your child has the necessary vaccinations for the destination country and carry any required medications. Verify that the child's medications are legal in the destination country.

Insurance

Obtain comprehensive travel insurance that covers the child and any potential medical needs during the trip.

Legal Advice

If there are existing family law orders or custody arrangements, consult with a legal professional to ensure compliance with all legal obligations before travelling.

By meticulously addressing both legal and emotional aspects, you can ensure a safe and comfortable travel experience for your child. Always stay informed about the latest regulations and maintain open communication with all parties involved to facilitate a smooth journey.

| 26 |

The Different Roles and Positions in Court.

During a divorce involving child custody in the **Federal Circuit and Family Court of Australia**, you will likely meet many new professionals and court officials.

Each plays an important role in the legal process, and understanding their responsibilities can help you feel more confident and informed as you navigate the system.

Here's a guide to the key people you're likely to come across, along with their responsibilities in relation to you.

Judge (or Magistrate)

The **Judge** (or **Magistrate** in some lower courts) is the primary decision-maker in your case. Their responsibilities include...

Conducting hearings
The judge listens to the evidence presented by both parties and their legal representatives.

Making rulings

They apply the law to your situation, making decisions on key issues such as child custody (parenting arrangements), property settlements, spousal maintenance, and other family law matters.

Issuing orders

Judges issue legally binding **court orders** that outline the decisions they've made. For example, they may issue parenting orders detailing the custody arrangements for children.

The judge's main responsibility in child custody matters is to determine what is in the **best interests of the child**, which is the guiding principle in all family law decisions.

Family Consultant (Family Report Writer)

A **family consultant** is a professional, often a psychologist or social worker, who assists the court by providing an independent assessment of the family dynamics and making recommendations regarding the child's best interests. Their responsibilities include...

Interviewing parents and children

The consultant will speak to each parent and the child to assess the family situation.

Writing a family report

Based on their assessments, they prepare a **family report** that includes recommendations to the court about parenting arrangements. The report can carry significant weight in the judge's decision-making process.

Providing expert opinions

Family consultants may give evidence in court and clarify their recommendations.

It's important to approach meetings with family consultants honestly and cooperatively, as their reports can significantly influence the court's decisions regarding custody.

Independent Children's Lawyer (ICL)

An Independent Children's Lawyer (ICL) is appointed by the court to represent the **best interests of the child** in complex cases. Their duties include…

Gathering information

The ICL may speak with the parents, the child, teachers, and other professionals (such as doctors) to gather a full understanding of the child's situation.

Making recommendations

Based on the information gathered, the ICL will make independent recommendations to the court about what they believe is in the child's best interests.

Presenting the child's perspective

While the ICL advocates for the child's best interests, they also ensure that the court hears the child's views, where appropriate.

The ICL acts independently and does not take sides with either parent. They focus solely on what will serve the child's welfare and well-being.

Your Lawyer (Family Law Solicitor and/or Barrister)

If you have legal representation, your **family law solicitor** or **barrister** will be your primary advocate throughout the court process. Their responsibilities include...

Providing legal advice

Your lawyer will advise you on your rights and options, helping you understand the likely outcomes of your case.

Preparing legal documents

They will draft and submit affidavits, applications, and other legal documents on your behalf.

Representing you in court

Your lawyer will present your case in court, argue on your behalf, and challenge the other party's evidence.

Negotiating settlements

In many cases, your lawyer will attempt to negotiate with the other party to reach an agreement without the need for a full trial.

In some instances, a **barrister** may represent you in court, particularly for more complex or contested matters. Your solicitor typically manages the case, while the barrister handles in-court advocacy.

The Other Party's Lawyer

If your ex-partner has legal representation, you will interact with their lawyer as well. The **other party's lawyer** will...

Represent your ex-partner's interests

They will advocate for their client and present evidence and arguments that support their case.

Negotiate with your lawyer

Much of the communication between you and your ex-partner, especially regarding negotiations and settlements, will occur through your respective lawyers.

Maintaining professionalism during these interactions, even through your lawyer, is important to ensure that negotiations are productive and constructive.

Court Registrar

A **court registrar** is a court officer who manages procedural aspects of your case and conducts hearings related to the progress of the case. Their responsibilities include...

Conducting directions hearings

Registrars often oversee procedural hearings (such as **directions hearings**) where they set timetables for the case, including deadlines for filing documents.

Approving consent orders

If both parties agree on issues like property division or child custody, the registrar may approve these **consent orders** without needing a judge to intervene.

Managing case flow

Registrars ensure that the case progresses through the court system smoothly and efficiently.

While registrars don't make decisions on the substantive issues in the case, they play a key role in managing its administrative aspects.

Family Dispute Resolution Practitioner (Mediator)

Before taking matters to court, parties are often encouraged (and in some cases, required) to attend **Family Dispute Resolution (FDR)**. A **Family Dispute Resolution Practitioner (FDRP)**, also known as a **mediator**, facilitates discussions between the parties to resolve disputes without going to court. Their responsibilities include...

Facilitating communication
The mediator helps both parties discuss their issues in a structured and respectful way.

Encouraging compromise
Mediators aim to help the parties reach mutually agreeable solutions on issues such as parenting arrangements and property division.

Providing certificates
If mediation is unsuccessful, the mediator may issue a **Section 60I certificate**, which is necessary before you can file for parenting orders in court.

Mediators do not take sides or make decisions for you. Instead, they guide the parties toward resolving their disputes independently.

Expert Witnesses (Psychologists, Financial Experts...)

In some cases, **expert witnesses** may be called to provide specialised opinions on key issues, such as a child's psychological needs or the valuation of complex assets. Their responsibilities include...

Providing independent assessments
Experts, such as psychologists or financial experts, may assess the family's situation and provide reports to the court.

Giving testimony
In some cases, experts may be asked to testify in court to explain their findings and recommendations.

Offering specialised insight
Experts help the court understand complex issues that require professional expertise beyond the knowledge of the parties or lawyers.

Expert opinions can carry significant weight, particularly in cases involving the mental health of children or disputes over large financial assets.

Court Security Personnel

When attending court, you will encounter **court security personnel** who are responsible for maintaining order and ensuring the safety of all individuals present in the court. Their responsibilities include...

Conducting security checks
They may check bags or scan individuals before entering the courtroom to ensure safety.

Maintaining order
In cases involving high conflict, security personnel may assist in managing interactions between parties or preventing disruptions.

If there are concerns about family violence, security personnel are particularly important in ensuring a safe environment within the courthouse.

Support People

You may bring a **support person** with you to court. This could be a friend, family member, or professional (such as a support worker) who provides emotional support throughout the legal process. Support people...

Offer comfort
Their presence can help reduce anxiety and provide moral support during stressful court proceedings.

Remain silent
Support people cannot speak on your behalf or engage with the court, but they can sit with you to offer encouragement.

In some cases, especially those involving family violence or intense emotional strain, having a support person can be invaluable.

In Summary

When going through divorce and child custody matters in the Federal Family Court, you will encounter many professionals, each with distinct roles and responsibilities.

From the judge who makes the final decision to the family consultant who provides expert assessments, understanding the functions of these individuals can help you feel more confident as you navigate the legal process.

Being aware of their responsibilities in relation to you will also help you better engage with the system and work towards achieving the best possible outcome for your case.

| 27 |

Helpful Resources.

This book is built on a foundation of general knowledge, personal experiences, and a deep understanding of the challenges faced by individuals navigating the family law system.

It draws from widely accepted principles of family law while weaving in personal narratives to offer practical, empathetic guidance. My goal is to provide you with clarity and confidence as you face the complexities of family law.

To be clear, this book **"Does Not Constitute Legal Advice"**.

While it provides valuable insights and practical tips, it is meant to inform and empower you, not replace the advice of a qualified legal professional.

Starting the Journey with Confidence

Stepping into the family law system can feel like stepping into the unknown. If this is your first experience with lawyers, courts, or legal processes, it's natural to feel uncertain.

My advice? **Start small and take one step at a time.**

Begin by seeking basic legal advice from reliable resources like a Community Legal Centre or Legal Aid. These organisations are equipped to provide free or low-cost consultations tailored to your circumstances.

Simultaneously, reach out to emotional and practical support services. Many of these services are designed to help people just like you and can offer the tools you need to navigate this challenging time.

There are people and organisations that want to help you succeed. Lean on them. Build your support network, ask questions, and don't hesitate to seek clarity where needed. The first step may feel intimidating, but it's also the most empowering setting the foundation for a more informed and confident journey.

Staying Informed

Family law is complex, and every situation is unique. It's vital to stay informed about your rights and responsibilities by relying on accurate, up-to-date information. Always turn to official sources such as government websites and legal professionals to guide your decisions.

While social media platforms may seem like convenient sources of information, they are often unreliable and emotionally charged. Many posts, though well-meaning, can stir bias and opinion, which may not align with the legal framework you need to follow.

Support Services for Navigating Family Law

Navigating family law can feel overwhelming at times, particularly for those with no prior experience dealing with police, lawyers, or courts. However, with the right resources and support, you can move through this process with clarity and confidence. This book aims to provide you with the guidance you need to take those critical first steps.

*"Your Decisions Must Be Based On
The Law as It Stands,*

Not On the Opinions of Others".

Graham McFarland

Legal Advice and Assistance

Community Legal Centres (CLCs):
These centres provide free legal advice, information, and referrals.

They are a good starting point for understanding your legal rights and obligations.

Visit the National Association of Community Legal Centres (clcs.org.au) to locate your nearest centre.

Legal Aid Commissions:
Offer free or low-cost legal assistance for those who qualify.

Services include advice, representation, and mediation in family law matters.

Visit legalaid.gov.au for state-specific information.

Family Advocacy and Support Services (FASS):
A specialised service that provides legal and social support for families involved in family law matters, particularly those affected by family violence.

Find more at your local Family Court or Federal Circuit Court.

MyGov:
Centralised access to government services, including Centrelink for financial support. (my.gov.au)

Emotional and Practical Support
Counselling and Mental Health Services

Relationships Australia
Offers counselling, family dispute resolution, and support groups.
relationships.org.au

Beyond Blue
Provides mental health support, particularly for those feeling overwhelmed. Call 1300 22 4636 or visit
beyondblue.org.au

Lifeline
A 24/7 crisis support hotline. Call 13 11 14.

Parenting Support

Parentline
Offers confidential parenting advice.
Available in most states (e.g., 1300 30 1300 in QLD/NT or 1300 130 052 in NSW).

Financial Counselling

National Debt Helpline
Free financial counselling for those struggling with the financial impact of separation. Call 1800 007 007 or visit
ndh.org.au

Mediation and Dispute Resolution

Family Dispute Resolution (FDR):
Mediation is a required step before most family law applications involving parenting.

Accredited providers include Relationships Australia and private FDR practitioners listed on the Attorney-General's Department website

ag.gov.au

Family Relationship Centres (FRCs):
Operated by the Australian Government, these centres offer information, mediation, and referrals.
familyrelationships.gov.au

Police and Safety Services

Domestic Violence Support 1800RESPECT
A confidential service providing support for those experiencing domestic violence. Call 1800 737 732 or visit
1800respect.org.au

Local Police
Many are hesitant to approach the police, but in cases of immediate danger or to enforce restraining orders, they are a vital resource.

Call 000 in emergencies or visit your local station for non-urgent matters.

Women's Legal Services:
Specialized in supporting women in family violence and family law matters.
Each state has its own service
e.g., Women's Legal Service NSW at wlsnsw.org.au

Support for Men

MensLine Australia:
Provides telephone and online counselling for men facing separation, parenting, or relationship challenges.
Call 1300 78 99 78 or visit mensline.org.au.

Dads in Distress:
A peer-support network for separated fathers. Visit parentsbeyondbreakup.com.

Below is a list of trusted government websites that provide comprehensive resources related to family law in Australia.

Family Law Act 1975:
The legislation that outlines parental responsibility and provides guidance on how decisions are made in the child's best interests.
www8.austlii.edu.au/cgi-bin/viewdb/au/legis/cth/consol_act/fla1975114/

Family Court of Western Australia:
Information and resources for family law matters in WA. WA is the only state that is unique, not aligning to the Family Law ACT of 1975.
www.familycourt.wa.gov.au

Attorney-General's Department – Family Law:
Legal information on family law, marriage, and relationship breakdowns.
www.ag.gov.au/families-and-marriage

Legal Aid Australia:
Aids and advice for family law matters.
www.legalaid.gov.au

Family Relationships Online:
A government resource for parenting plans, separation, and mediation.
www.familyrelationships.gov.au

Federal Circuit and Family Court of Australia (FCFCOA):
The court's website provides information on parental responsibility and how parenting orders are decided:
www.fcfcoa.gov.au/fl/parenting-orders

Services Australia (Child Support)
for official guidelines and tools:
www.servicesaustralia.gov.au/child-support

Australian Taxation Office (ATO):
Provides information on the taxation implications of superannuation splitting during divorce or separation.
www.ato.gov.au/forms-and-instructions/capital-gains-tax-guide-2023/part-a-about-capital-gains-tax/marriage-or-relationship-breakdown

And sites for Travelling

Smartraveller
When travelling with children there are laws around children travelling without both parents. Airlines also have rules you must follow. Travelling with only one parent. You may need extra documents if only one parent is travelling. Particularly if you don't have the same surname as your child.

www.smartraveller.gov.au/before-you-go/who-you-are/children

Australian Passport Office

Incomplete consent, do you need an Australian court order that permits the child to have an Australian passport, travel internationally or live or spend time with a person outside Australia, a passport under the special circumstances.

www.passports.gov.au/IncompleteConsent

Federal Circuit Court

Children and international travel after family separation. If you consent to a child travelling out of Australia in the future or wish to take a child out of Australia yourself, you must apply to the Court (before you travel) to have the child's name removed from the Airport Watch List (if it's on it).

www.fcfcoa.gov.au/fl/pubs/children-international-travel

Consent Guide

Child Traveling with 1 Parent or Non-family Member? This form is particularly important for international travel. This link helps with the details that should be included in the consent form

www.ifly.com/flying-info-and-tips/flying-with-children/child-travel-consent

By using these resources, you can ensure that you are getting accurate information tailored to your specific situation, and you will feel more empowered as you navigate the family law system.

*"Remember,
you are Not Alone".*

Graham McFarland

| 28 |

"Hang in There"

As I come to the end of this book, I want to leave you with a message of hope and resilience. The journey through family law, with its complex emotions and legal challenges, can often feel overwhelming.

If my own experiences have taught me anything, it's that no matter how dark and difficult the storm, there is always a way through. I know this because I have walked this path myself.

I have experienced the heartbreak of family separation, the gut-wrenching pain of parental alienation, and the devastation that domestic violence brings.

There were times when it felt like the road ahead was insurmountable, when fear, frustration, and uncertainty were constant companions. But through all of those struggles, I found a way to not only survive but to build a life that is more fulfilling than I ever thought possible.

Today, my children are adults, and I am proud to say that we have a wonderful relationship. The bond we share, forged through the trials we faced, is something I treasure every day. I am also fortunate enough to be a grandfather, which is one of the greatest joys of my life. Watching my grandchildren grow has brought a new kind of fulfilment, a reminder that love and family, in all their forms, are the most important things we have.

And just as my family life has blossomed, so too has my personal life. After everything I went through, I am blessed to have found a partner who supports, loves, and complements me in ways I never could have imagined. Together, we have built a life that I once thought was out of reach—a life filled with love, laughter, and shared dreams.

I share my personal story with you not to diminish the very real and painful challenges that come with family law issues, but to remind you that there is life after hardship.

There is healing after the wounds, and there is 'light at the end of the tunnel'. Boy I use to hate and despise that quote, it always felt distant and unachievable… But it's true, its life!

Even when it seems like the situation is impossible, it's important to remember that your journey is not defined by the challenges you face but by how you choose to overcome them.

The experiences you are going through now are shaping you and, though it may not feel like it, they are also opening new possibilities. The strength you will gain from navigating these difficult moments will serve you in ways you can't yet see.

Whether you are dealing with separation, custody disputes, financial struggles, or the pain of alienation or abuse, know that you are capable of weathering the storm. You have the power to create a better future, not just for yourself but for your children, and to find peace and happiness beyond the difficulties.

In closing, I hope this book has provided you with the knowledge, tools, and encouragement you need to navigate your own family law journey. I want you to know that no matter where you are on this path, you are not alone. There is a community of people, like me, who have been through similar struggles and who are here to support you. Take heart in knowing that you have the strength to rebuild, to heal, and to thrive.

The journey is not easy, but it is one worth taking. I wish you resilience, courage, and peace as you move forward, and I hope that, like me, you will come out the other side stronger, more fulfilled, and with a life that brings you happiness and joy.

With warmest regards and my heartfelt support.

Graham "GMAC" McFarland …. "PA"….

For Nearly Twenty Years

I have been privileged to serve as an advocate in the realm of family law, walking alongside countless families through one of the most emotionally charged and complex areas of their life.

As someone who has experienced family law up close - not from the position of a lawyer, but as a guide, a supporter, and sometimes a voice for those who struggle to find their own - this book represents my effort to share what I have learned and observed over these many years.

Family law in Australia, as in many parts of the world, is both an intricate legal framework and a deeply human process. It is shaped by the need to balance legal rights with human emotions, parental responsibilities with children's needs, and fairness with compassion.

This book is designed to inform, guide, and empower you as you navigate family law issues, so that you feel equipped to ask the right questions, understand your options, and make your own informed decisions.

Whether you're dealing with the breakdown of a relationship, child custody, property division, domestic violence, or other family-related matters, this book is here to provide clarity and a road map through what can often feel like an overwhelming and uncertain process.

Family law is not just about rules and regulations; it is about people, relationships, and, most importantly, families.

Each case is unique, and while the laws are designed to provide a structure for resolving disputes, they cannot account for the individual nuances of your personal experience.

I Have Written this Book

*Focused on a Non-Biased, Non-Gendered,
Zero Agenda Point of View.*

My Belief Has Been and Will <u>Always Be</u>!

*That all Children Deserve Both Parents
in Their Life.*

*Sadly,
Australian Political Prejudices and the Community
Do Not Allow This to Occur".*

Graham McFarland

WHO IS GRAHAM "GMAC" MCFARLAND?

The writer of this book is Graham McFarland, locally known as GMAC. Graham you could say is what you would now consider a common Australian man who married too early.

What Graham experienced after doing what he thought was the right thing, raise and provide for a family, is what led him to becoming an advocate for better family laws.

Marriage Breakdown

After his marriage broke down and separated, he moved his young family back to Sydney to a suburb called Glenwood, Northwest of Parramatta in NSW. This was for the benefit of the children being close to extended family and the proximity to the good local schools.

This separation led to financial destruction from the costs of child support, often consuming most of his income. This brought the onset of homelessness, with little to no support systems available, and not entitled to financial support, as he had a full-time job and was not entitled to government support.

This then led to parental alienation, over the initial years seldom seeing or spending quality time with his young children. The laws at the time were in favour of the mother as the custodial parent to the children.

In the mid 2000's Graham became heavily depressed, removed from fatherhood, missing out on his children growing up all because of separation and the communities bias that the parent will always be the mother.

The Power of Men Support Group's

Luckily, Graham is a fighter, this outcome just didn't sit well with him. He had a desire for a fairer outcome from family separation. After a few dyer years, he found the community "Dads in Distress" and spoke regularly to a man…. Tony Miller.

Tony and the "Dads in Distress" community were amazing, they gave purpose and belief that things will change…. That this was only a temporary setback. They enriched Graham with knowledge about law, support that was available and action plans for a better relationship with his children.

From that interaction, Graham became extremely focused on being the BEST dad he could ever be. First came his own well-being, fitness and mental growth. He read everything, the law, other family law cases and started engaging with like-minded people. This led to studying state and federal constitutional laws.

This personal growth saw Graham's career blossom, his health focus increase and his knowledge of his rights as an active parent increase. Eventually the tides started changing, he went from a few nights a month to 50/50 shared care. And in Graham's case eventually full care and the main carer of his children.

*"If only Governments
and Politicians,*

*Understood the Power of Support
for Men in the Community and the Economy"!*

Graham McFarland
Federal Candidate
Electorate of Greenway 2019

Community Advocacy

In the years 2015 – 2018, Graham was often seen standing outside the Parramatta Family Law courts, creating awareness around family law outcomes, especially supporting men going through the same journey.

He built a network of support around him. This created support mechanisms for parents, through his organisation "Family Crisis Support". This led to emergency accommodation options for men, because in Australia there are no emergency or domestic violence shelters for men.

His new network of Dads was able to resettle a separated father quickly, from temporary accommodation to finding more permanent solutions. His community was able to furnish these new homes through furniture donations. He also arranged free legal seminars and emergency food and petrol vouchers. This reduced the initial financial burden of men after separation.

During these times he learned very quickly how the community really worked, fighting often against dreaded prejudices of the last 2 decades.

The limited Politicians and Councillors who would listen would often be agreeable but would say, ...

"Family Law is a Nuclear Bomb".

What this meant was no politician wanted to fight for families, as it was taboo, and their political careers would be at risk. Many a meeting would end like this, especially as "off the record"...

Federal Election Candidate 2019

The catalyst for this whole experience was Graham and 6 other members from this community running for Parliament in the 2019 Federal Election. Graham fully funded his own campaign and spent 6 months walking the streets of his electorate, over 260 km's.

The focus of the team wasn't to get elected; they knew as independents it was almost impossible without a lot of money. But boy did it help the growing conversation…

Later that year, the government started to listen. With all the family law advocates from all over Australia getting involved, they all achieved a fantastic outcome.

Later that year, September 2019, Australian Prime Minister Scott Morrison started a new committee to look at the 60 recommendations made from the 2017 Family Law review, often coined the "Broken Family Law".

After 2 Decades

These days, Graham is now a grandfather, a young one at that. He has found a remarkable partner that he loves and adores, they got engaged this year on the banks of the Lough Derg, Youghalarra Ireland, His ancestral home.

He has been interviewed a few times, and still is active in his community. You will find him on community radio weekly, producing and broadcasting on community radio with two other remarkable dads, "The Dads Radio Show", a show of dads talking about all thing's fatherhood and life.…

The basis of this book was to share the questions that 1000's of men has asked him over the last decade.

Hopefully to share his positive and contagious attitude towards life to 1000's of more…

"The War you're Fighting
is not Against your Ex-partner or
the Legal System...

it's Against Despair, Hopelessness, and Fear".

"And that is a War You Can Win"!

Graham McFarland

SURVIVING SEPARATION

www.ingramcontent.com/pod-product-compliance
Lightning Source LLC
Chambersburg PA
CBHW052138070526
44585CB00017B/1874